Gates To The Garden

Adam Kremer

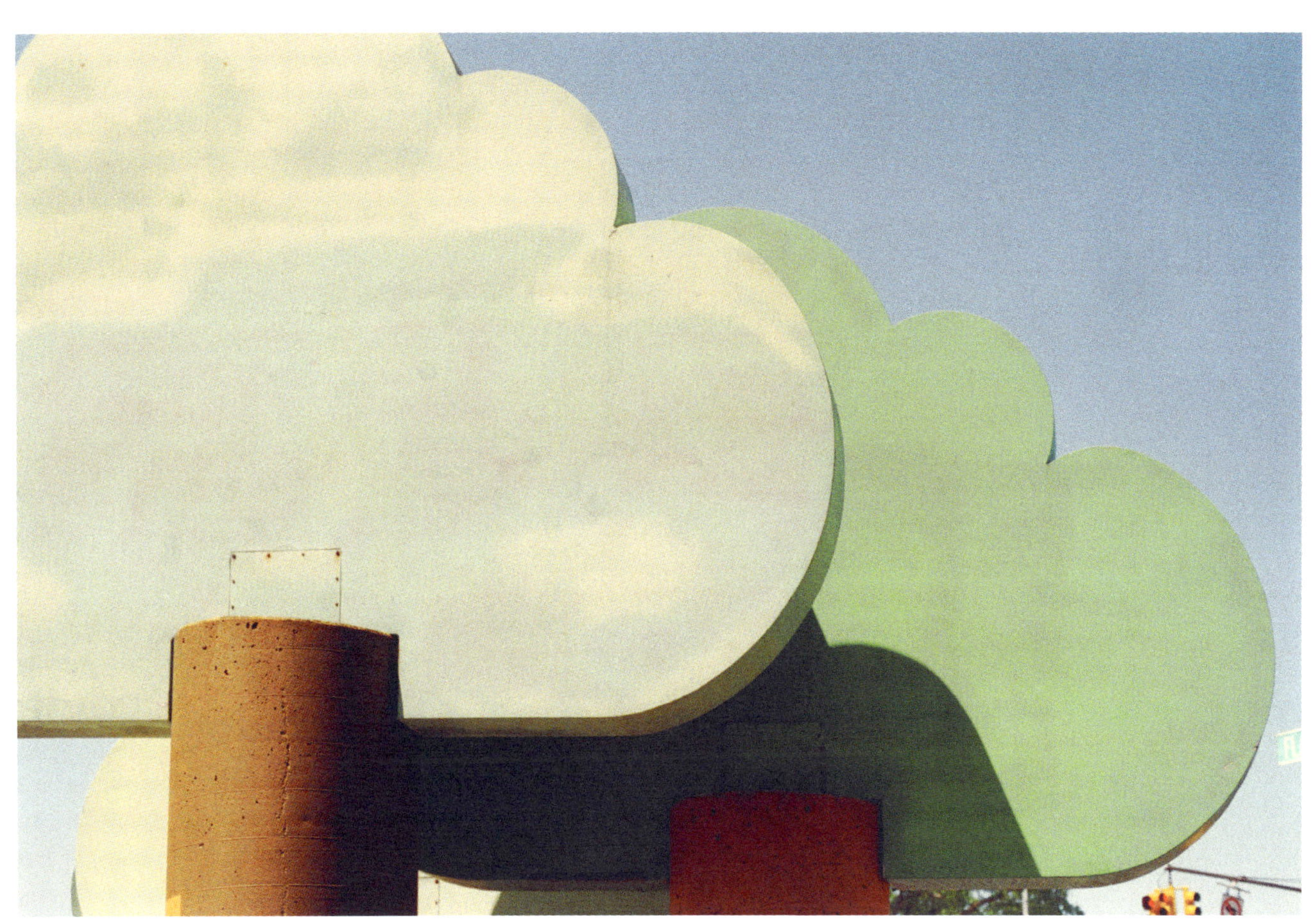

Indications of the Stirrings All Along

Jenni Crain

Maybe, by closing our eyes, we see more clearly. These constructs insinuate the secrets that the corner itself elucidates. These crossings outlive any attempts to capture. They clasp.

With cheek pressed to the pavement, the sun laps at the jointed dissonance. From overhead, the vibrations of brine and the intertidal meet in each direction. Anywhere, we remember the ways in which one tremble makes another known.

Want is an engagement. Tethered to the absorption of delight. Motivated, in part, by capricious currencies and the suspicion of dissolution. Galvanized by the gush of dependability.

When we lean, we rely. Up and against is osmosis. An entanglement whereby the given and the implied found the fabric of our fantasy. Rooted in the disposition of becoming.

In Adam Kremer's photography, the subject encapsulates the entirety of the scene and its representations. This depiction defies the seeming singularity of the photographic instance and exists, instead, within the totality of the historical trajectory of the subject's endurance. What we see is a signification of what we feel.

An airplane in its flight path appears to travel at a slower pace than a bird in flight. As a bird in flight aligns with its surrounding built and natural environment, it symbolizes the world's harmonic movements, at least, from a grounded vantage. An airplane in flight indicates this oscillation between a desire to unite and the distance defining these separate environments. Kremer's photographs make palpable this very distance and desire.

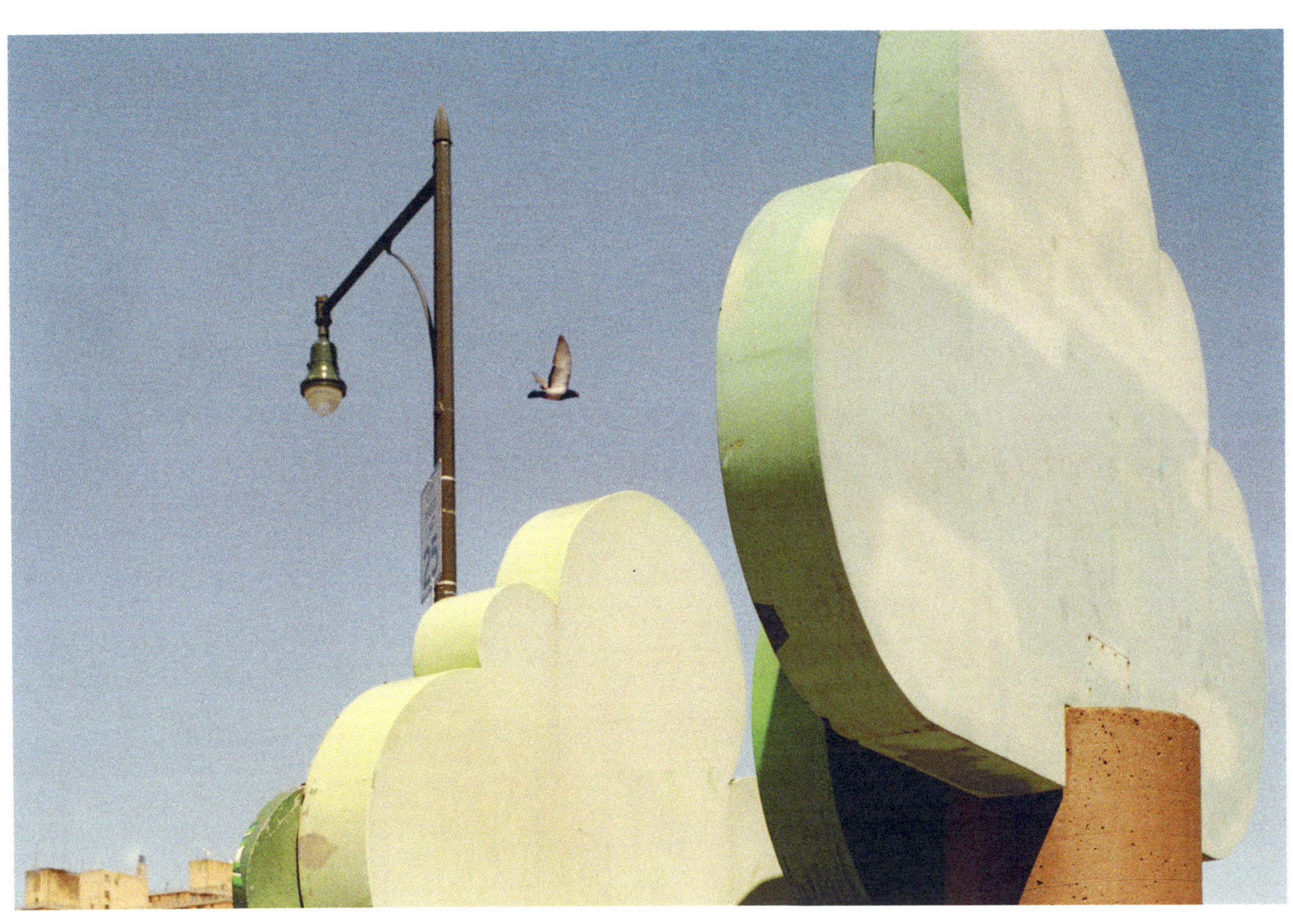

TO DO IS TO BE
SOCRATES
TO BE IS TO DO
PLATO
BE DO BE DO
sinatra

In the garden I am everything. I am leader and follower. I tend to the earth and take to my needs. I am the life between two moments measured by movement.

The history of photographing has slowly unfolded as a conflict of use and intent. Style matters only in its relation to application and content. My style is the act of photographing.

The image is the eyes' metaphor.
I am form as function.
I am body as shadow.

Everything begins with self. Images begin with the photographer and extend outwards to end with the subject. Photographs begin with the image and end with their suggested relationship to one and other. A photograph is completed by the distance between viewer and photographer. To view a photograph is to accept a great responsibility.

Photography is not made through a lens, but through fantasy. A photograph can be made without a lens, but not without distance or suggestion.

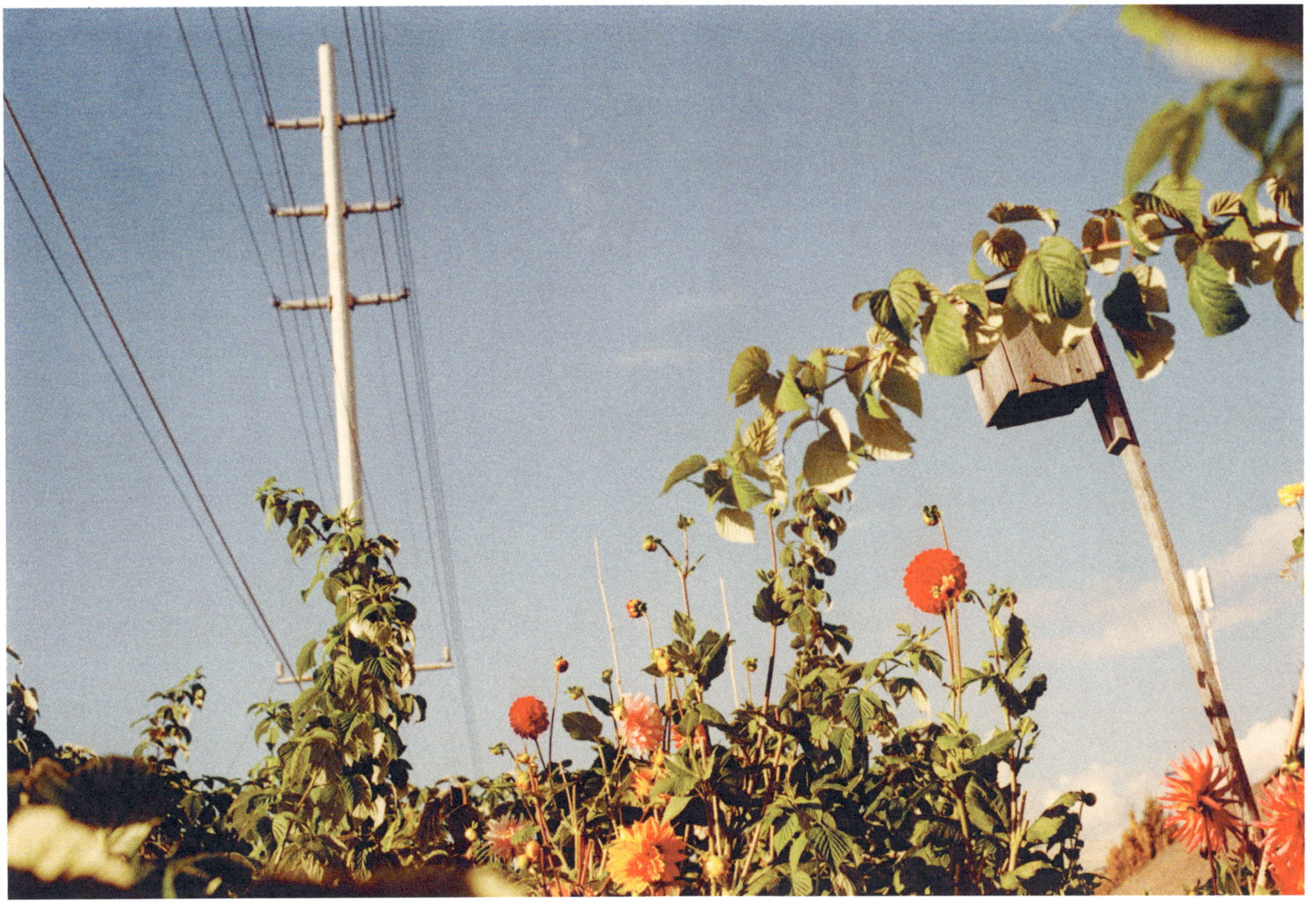

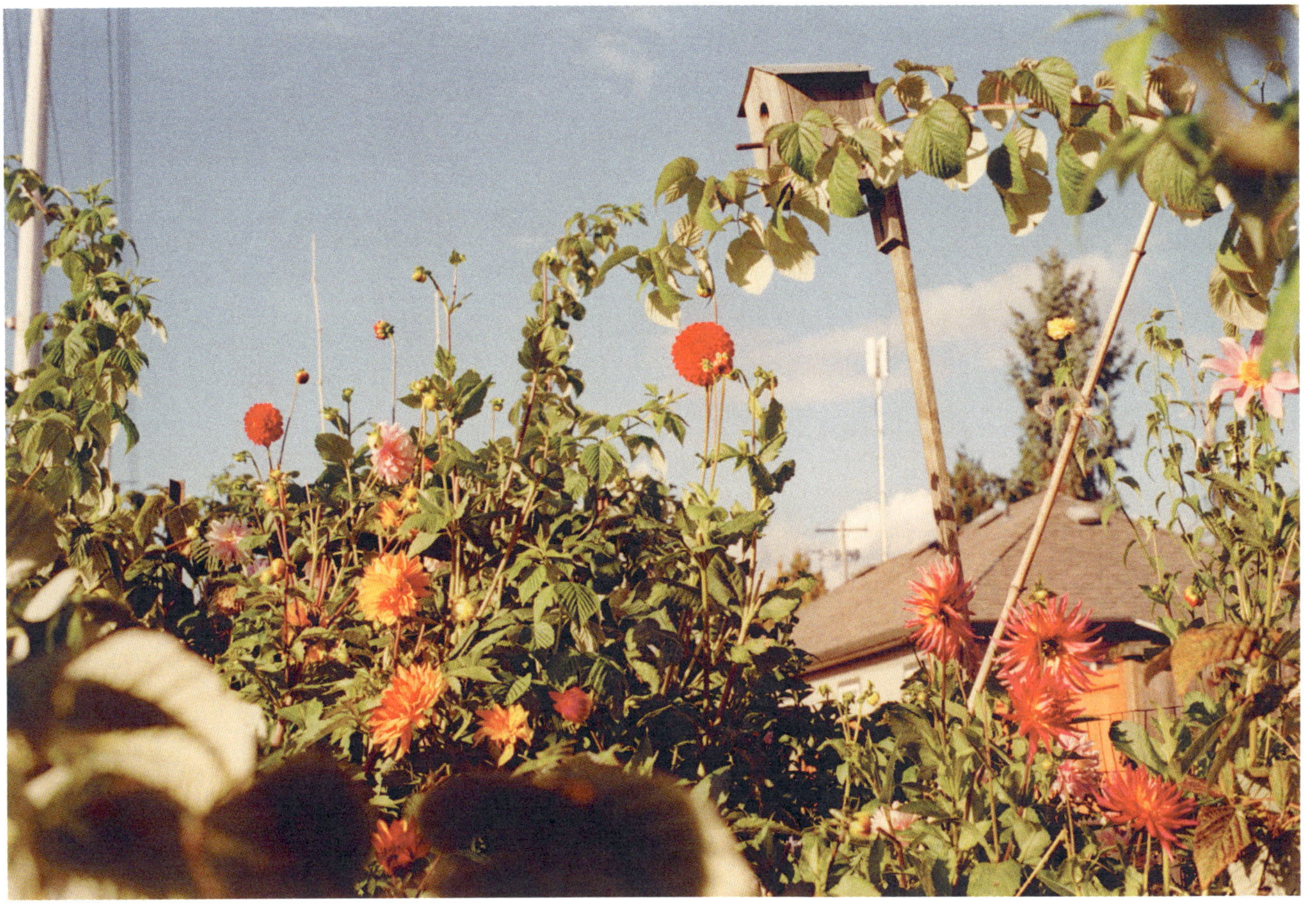

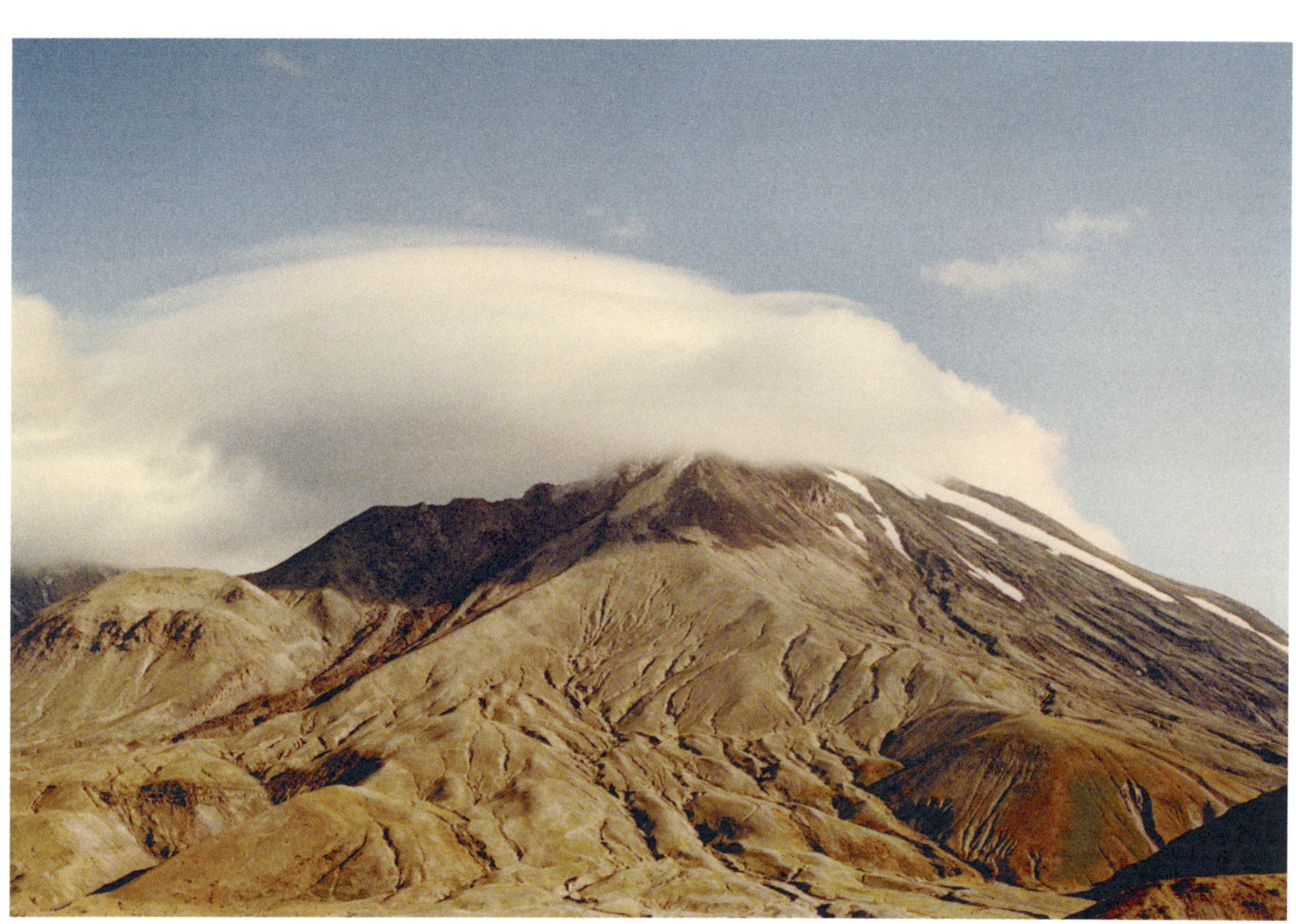

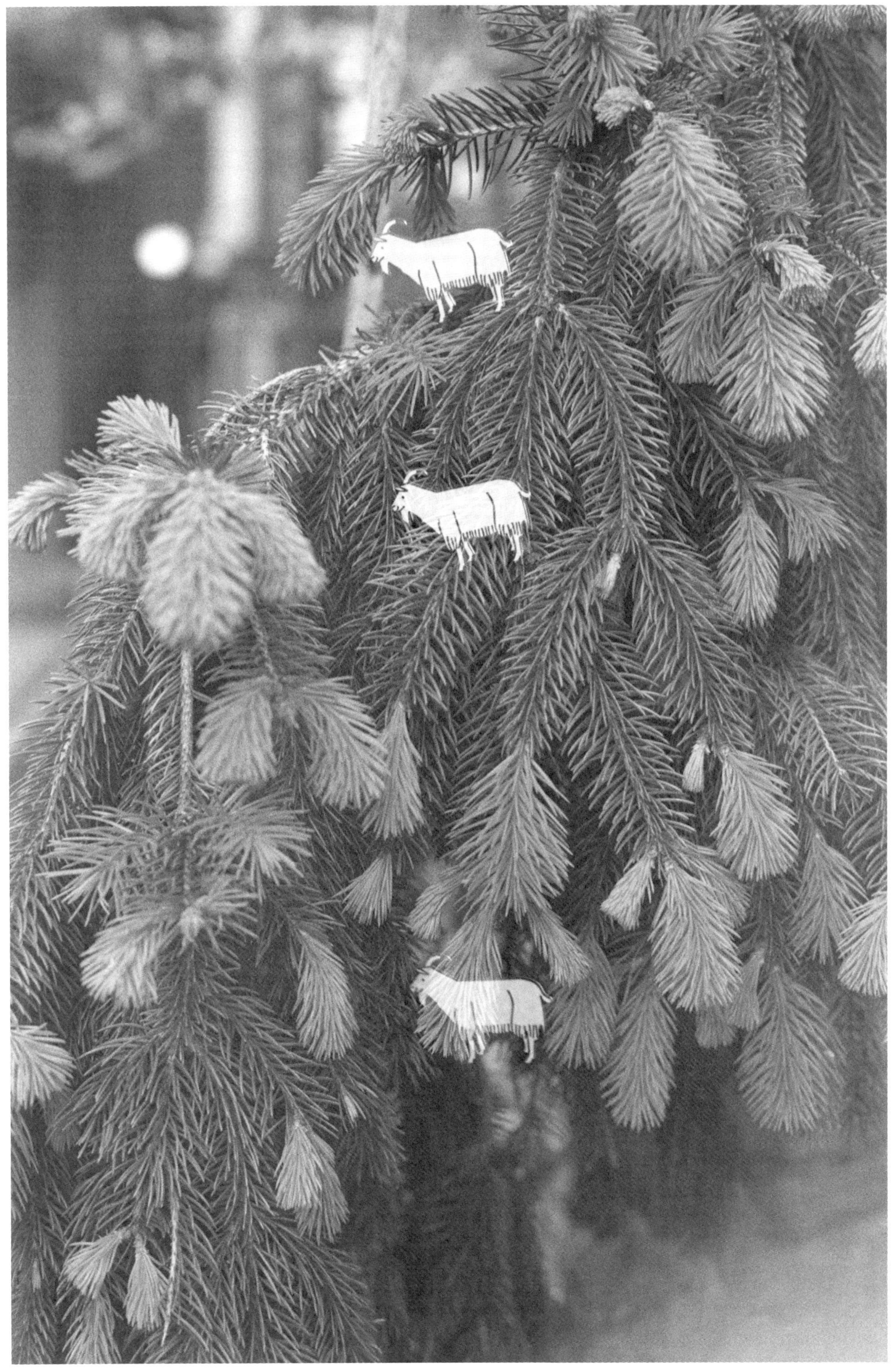

The garden is a utopian space, an intentional construction where man brings order to the natural world's chaos. The garden envelops the desire for control and understanding. It is an act of becoming.

The garden may be likened to the photographer's inventory. Material is gathered, arranged, and harvested. We tend to the garden and it provides us with the possibility of direction and meaning.

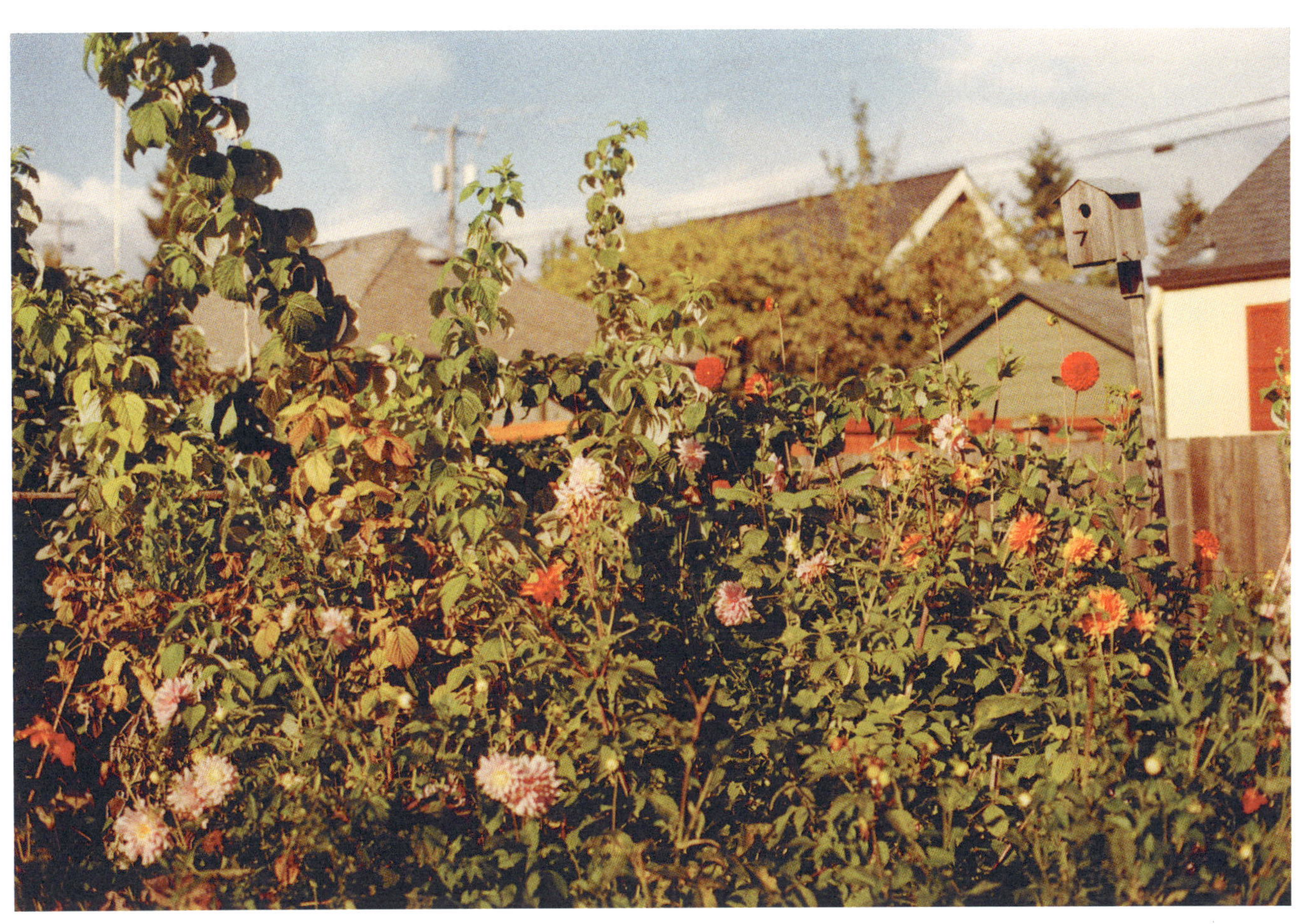

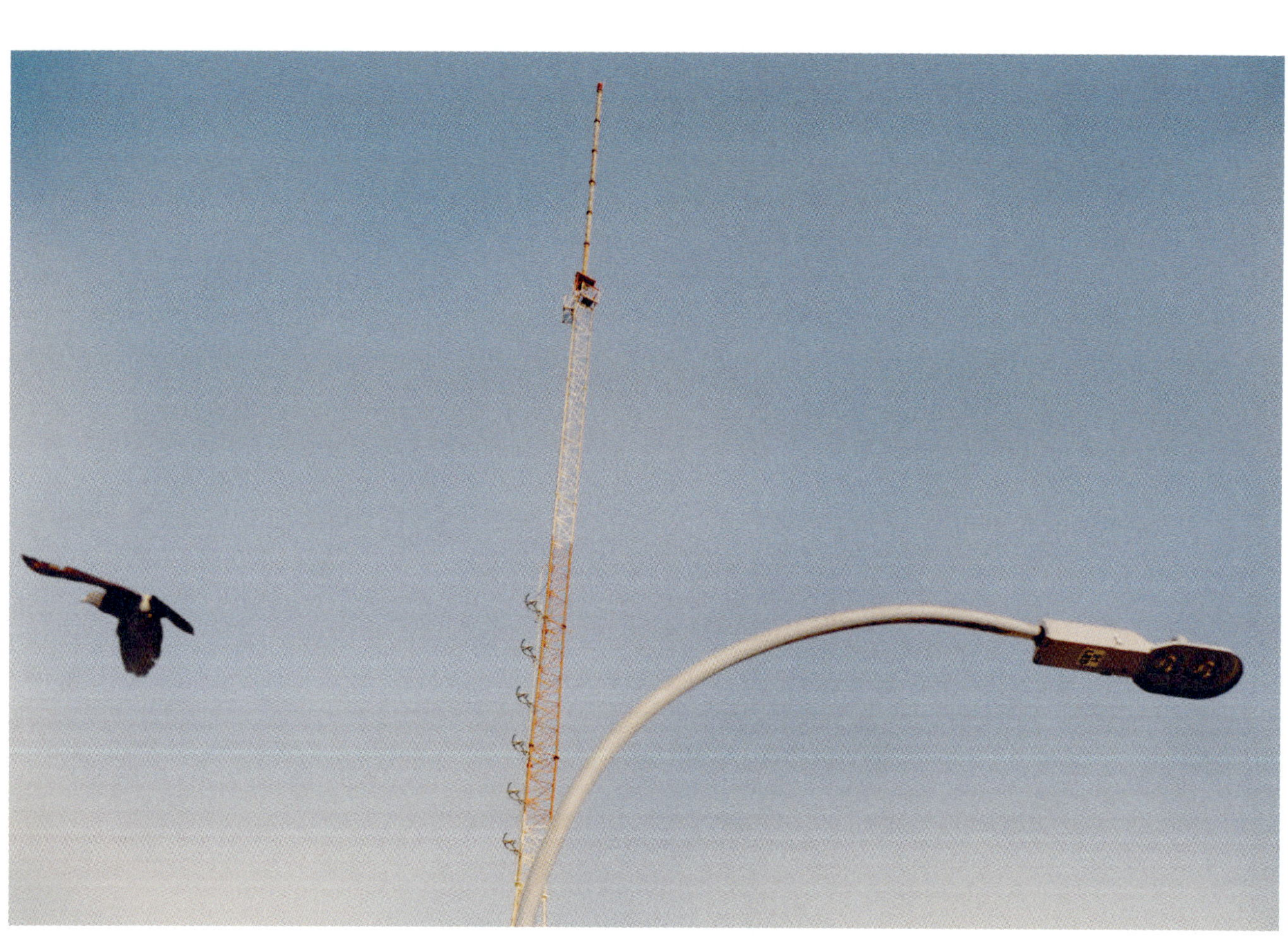

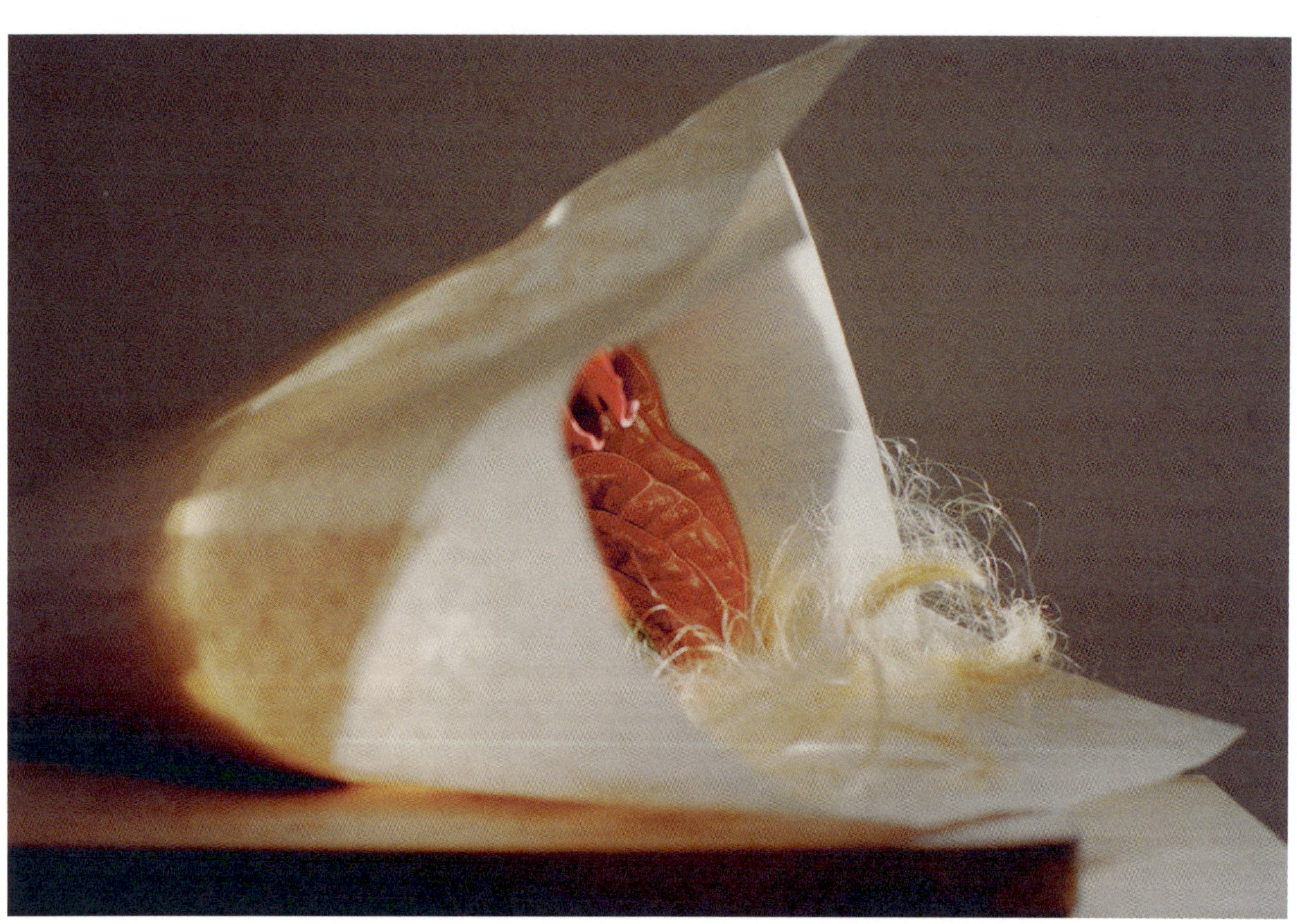

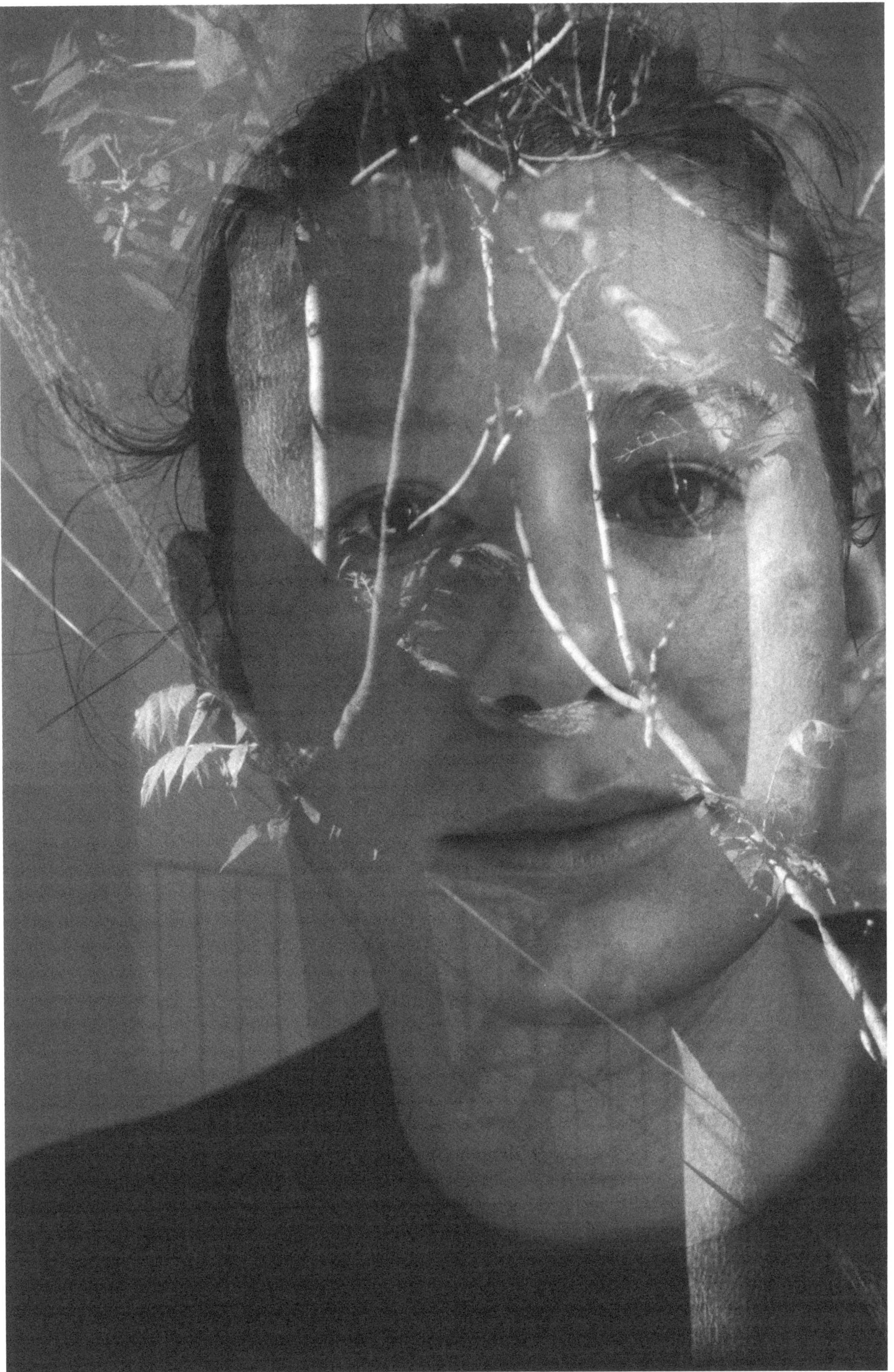

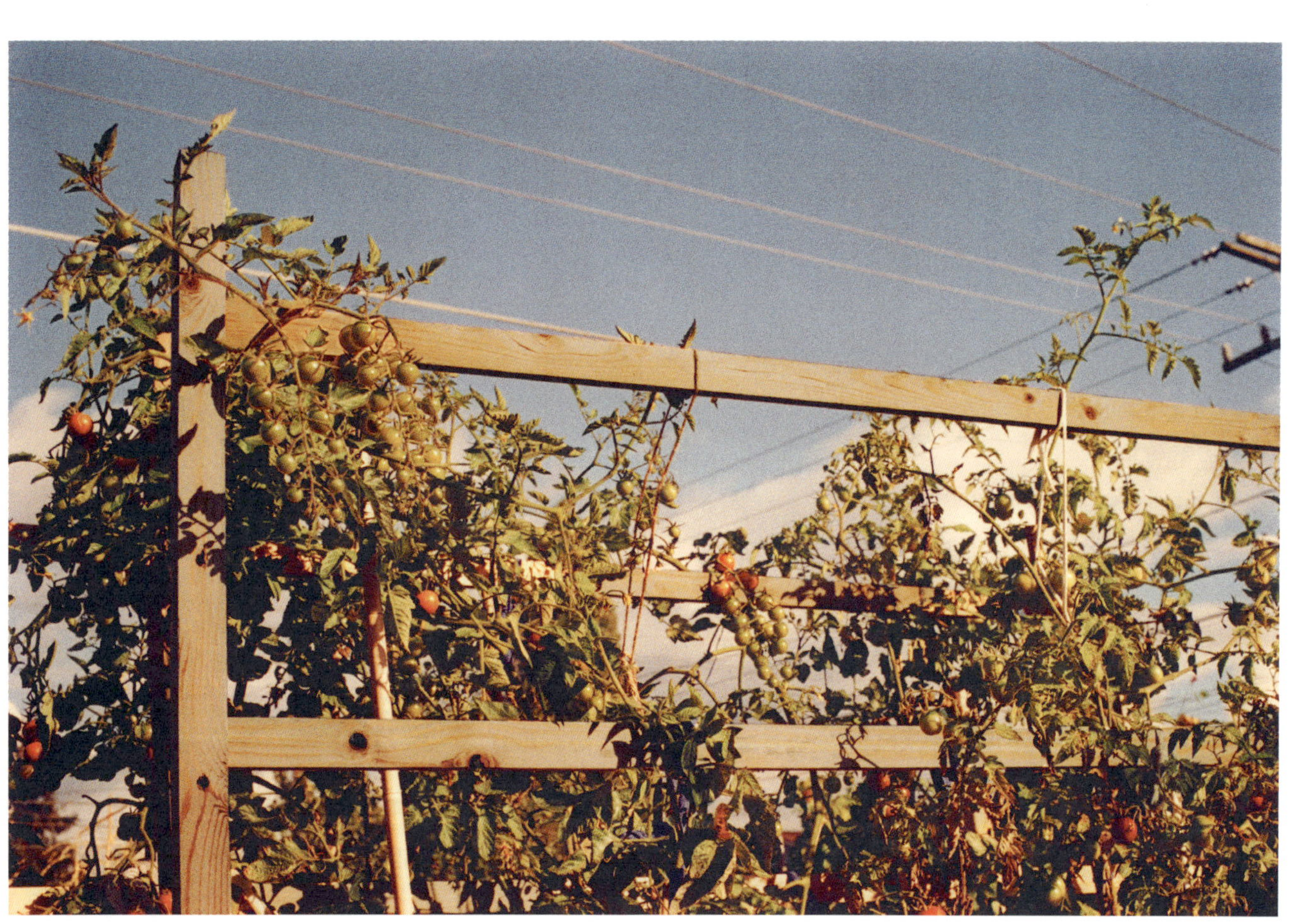

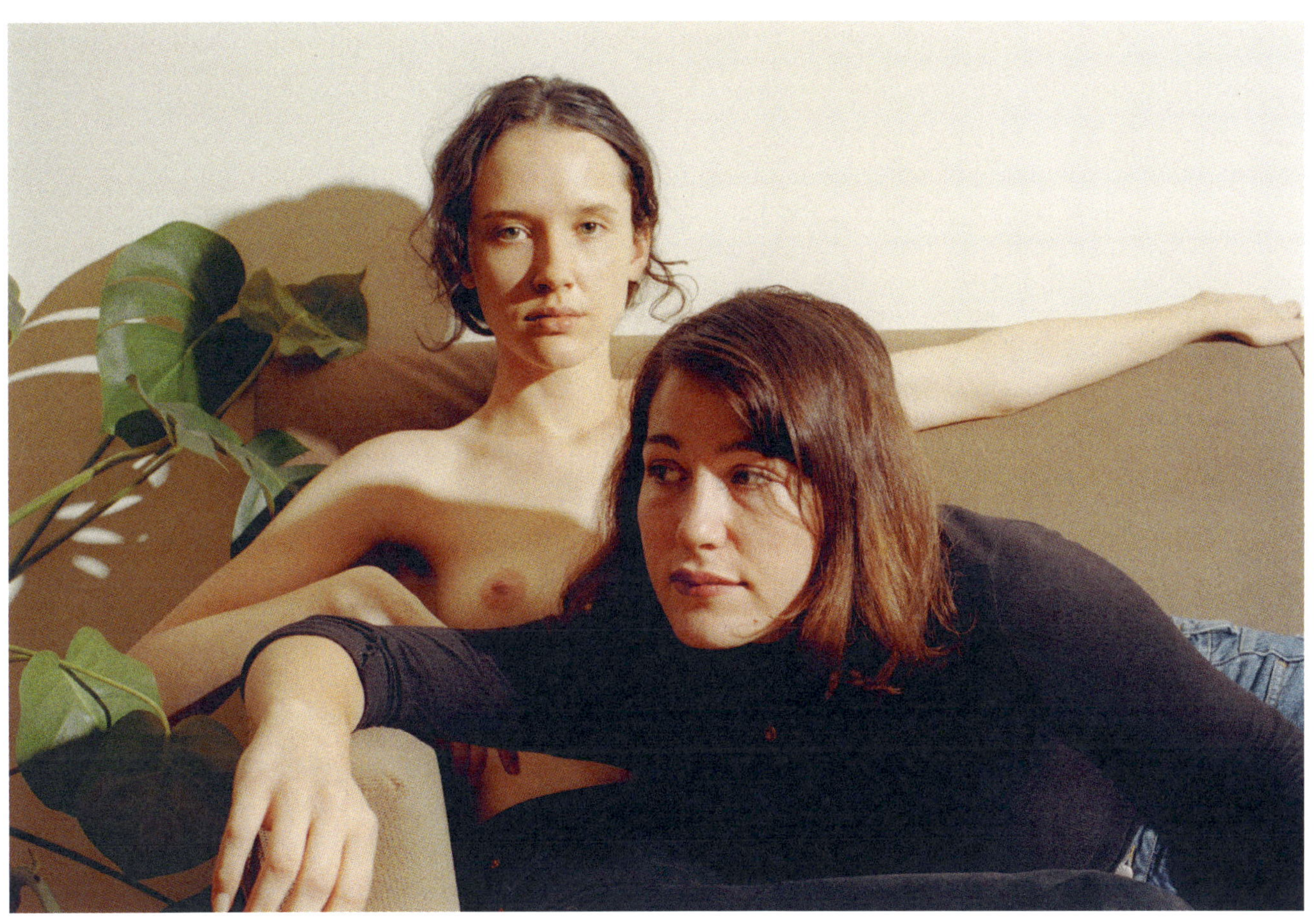

TO DO IS TO BE
SOCRATES
TO BE IS TO DO
PLATO
DO BE DO BE DO
Sinatra

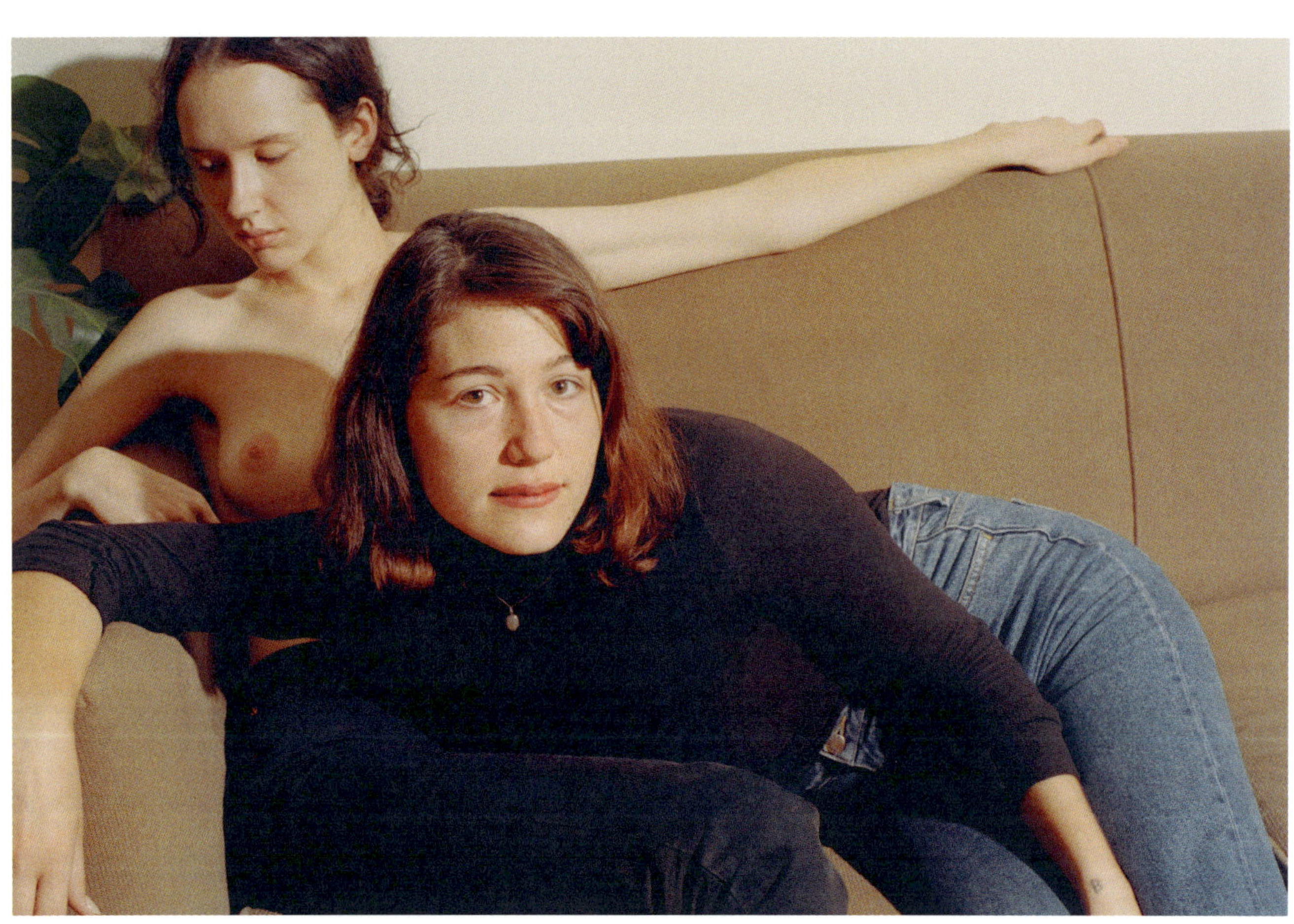

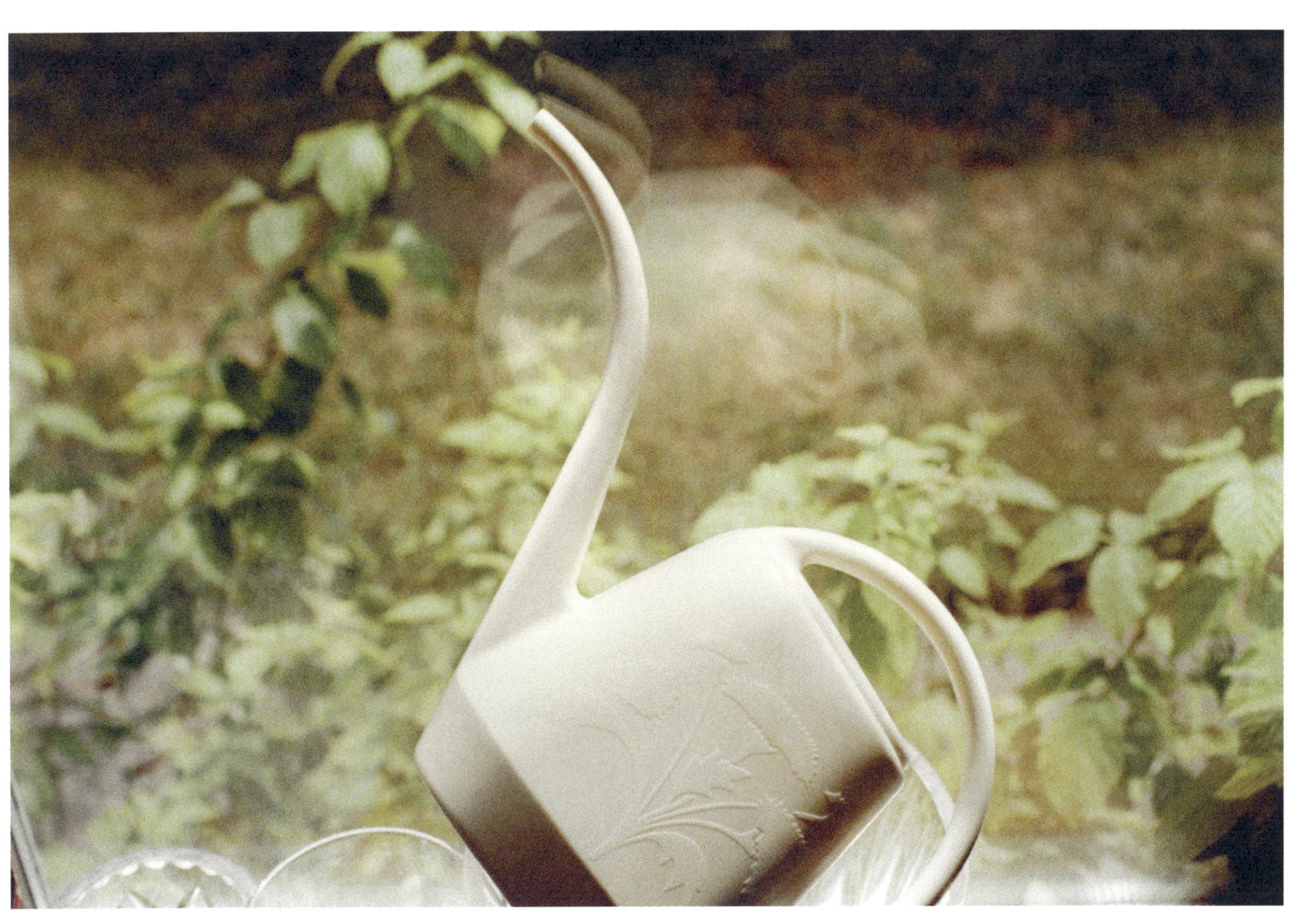

There is a bridge in Upstate New York which travels north and south. The bridge's arching length marks the point of crossing between two small towns. It also marks the point of convergence between salt water flowing in from the west, and fresh water flowing in from the east.

A still space is created between crossing traffic and converging water flow, a space which is simultaneously above, below, and in all cardinal directions.

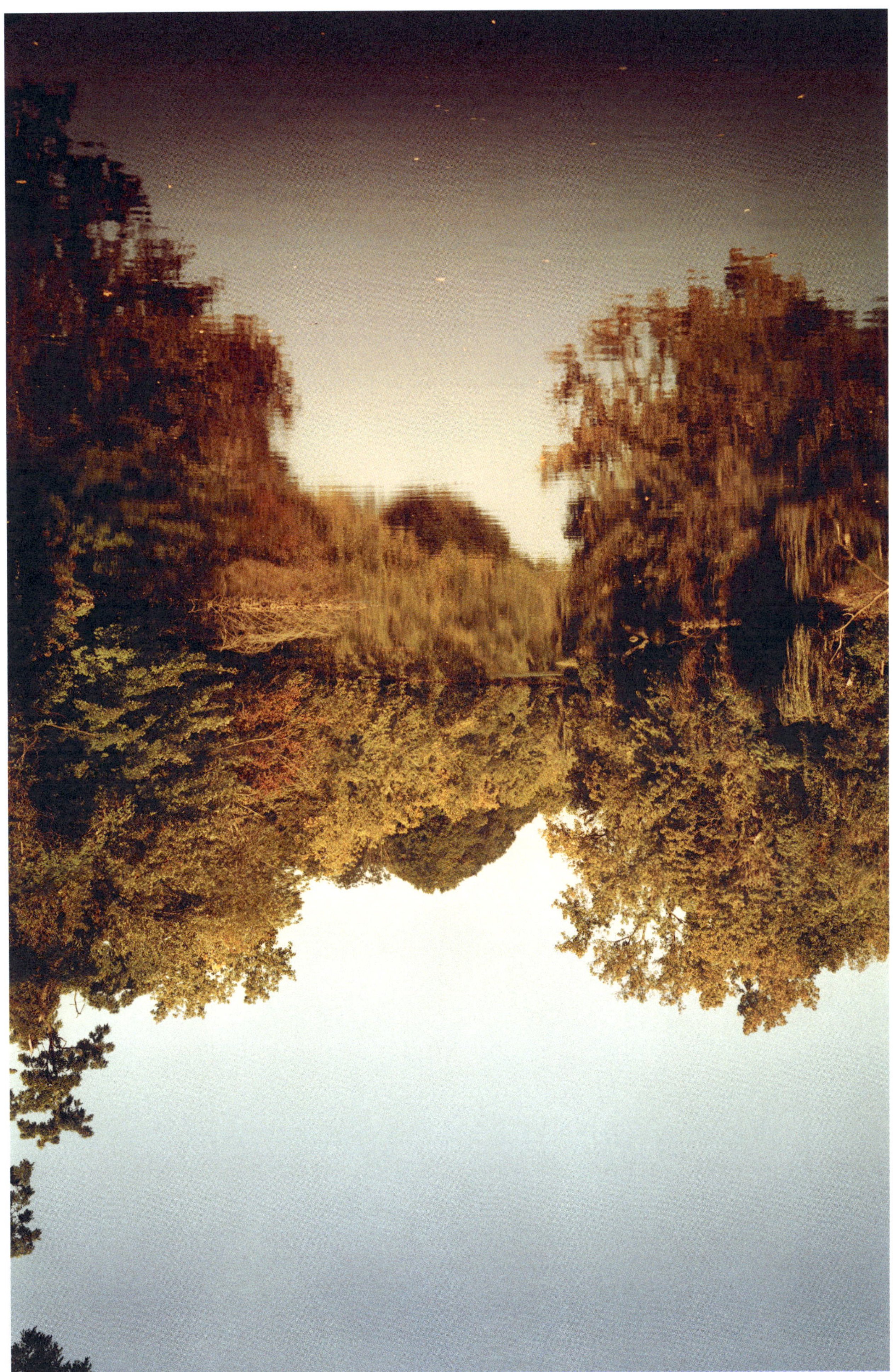

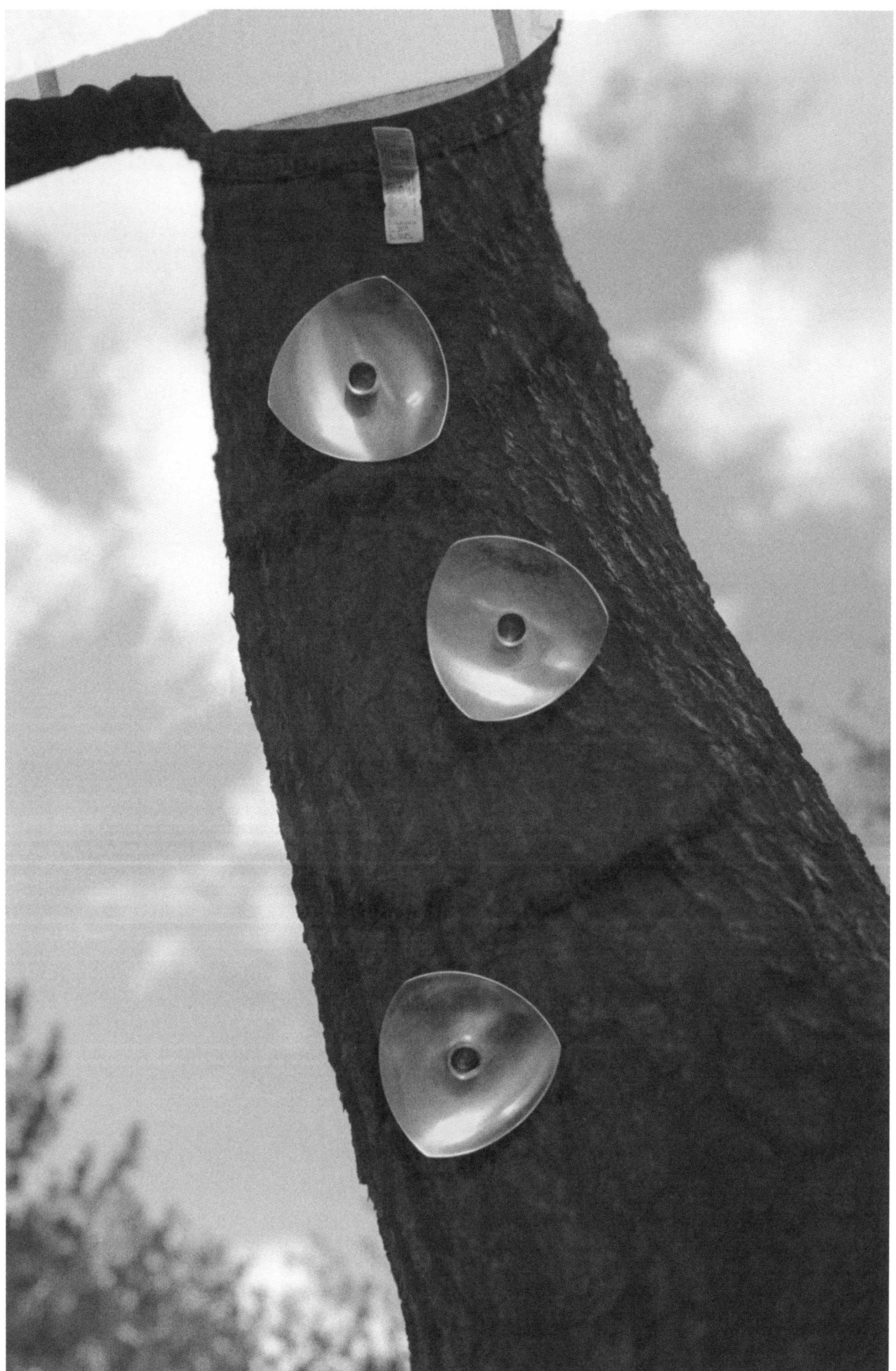

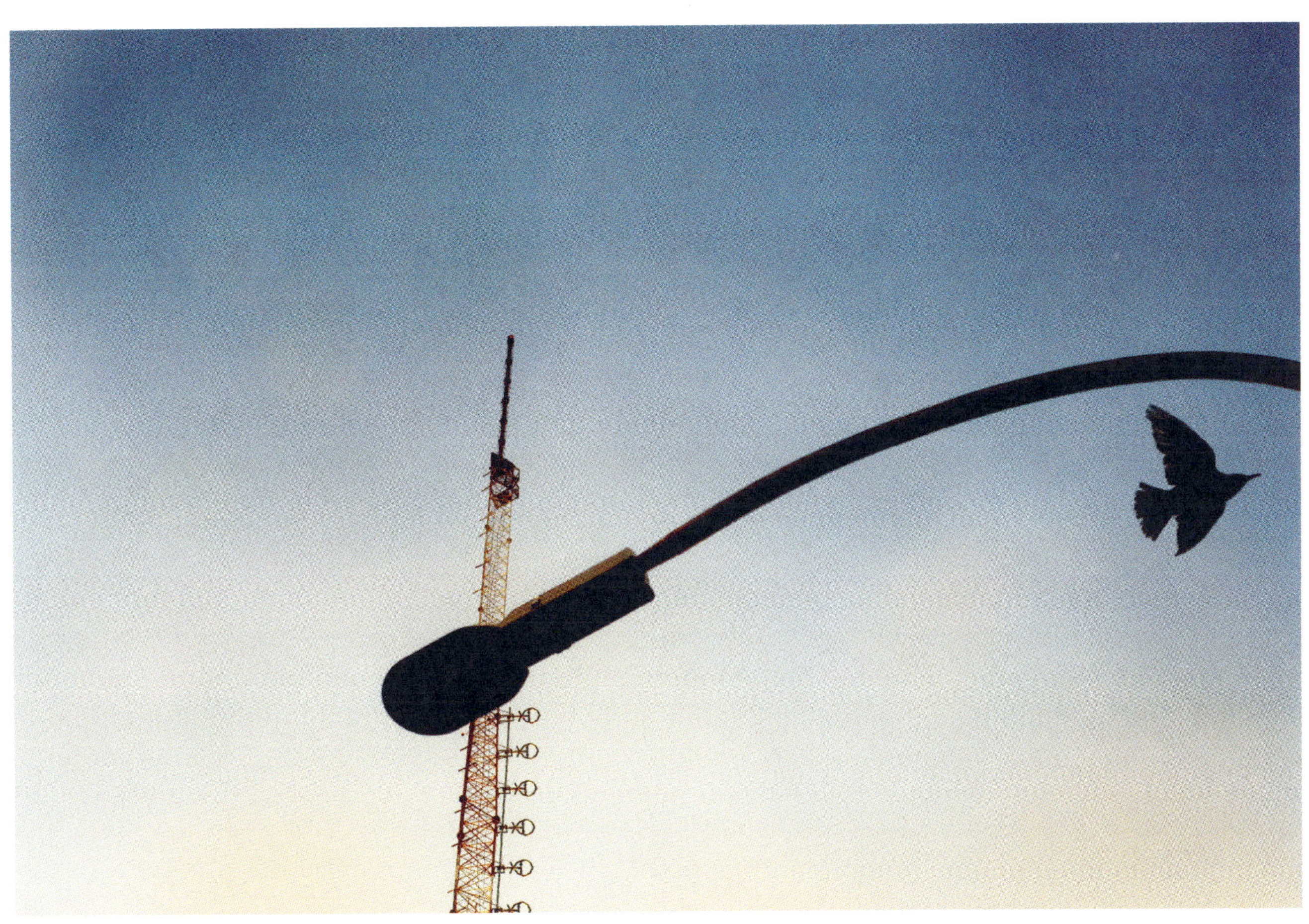

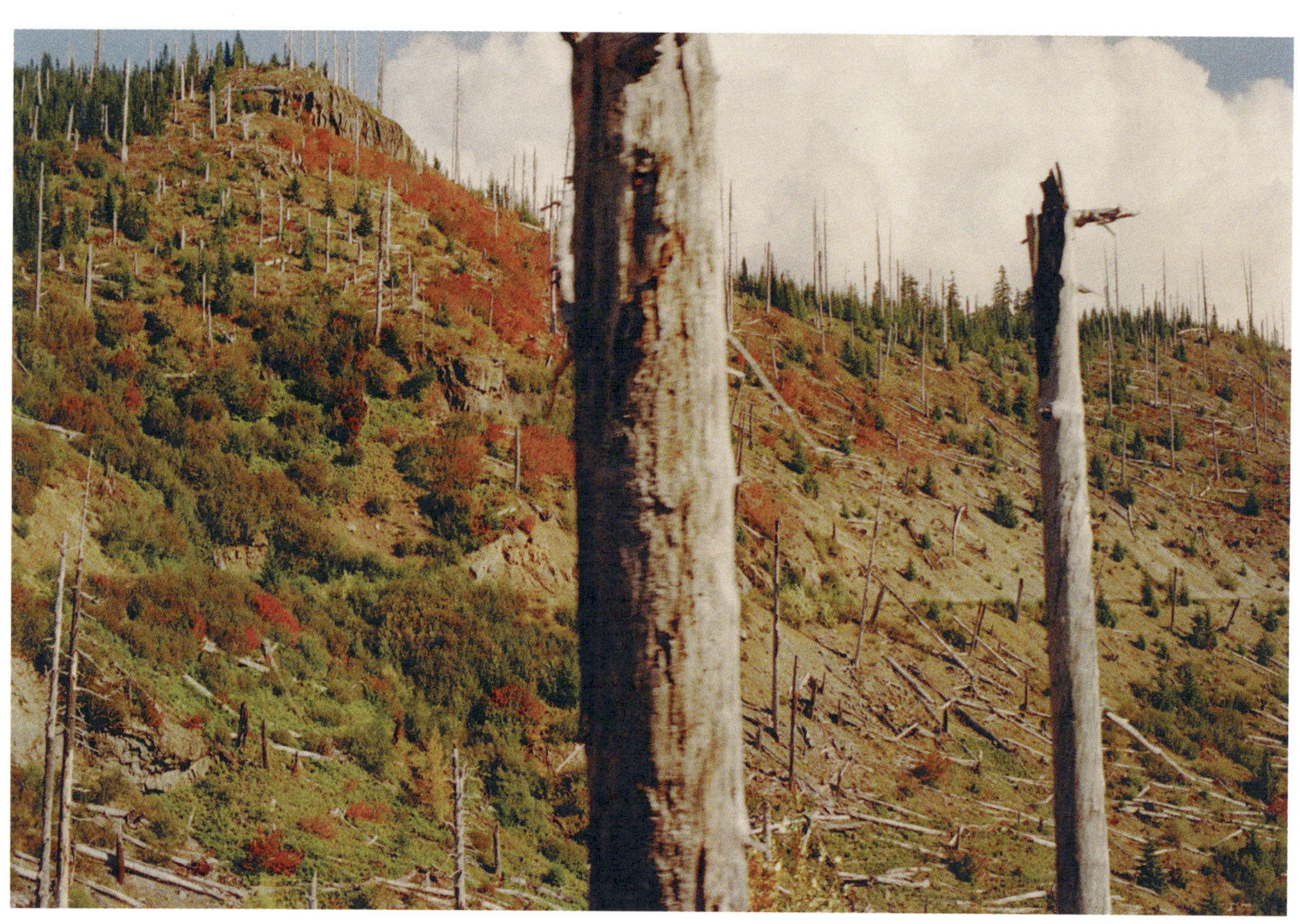

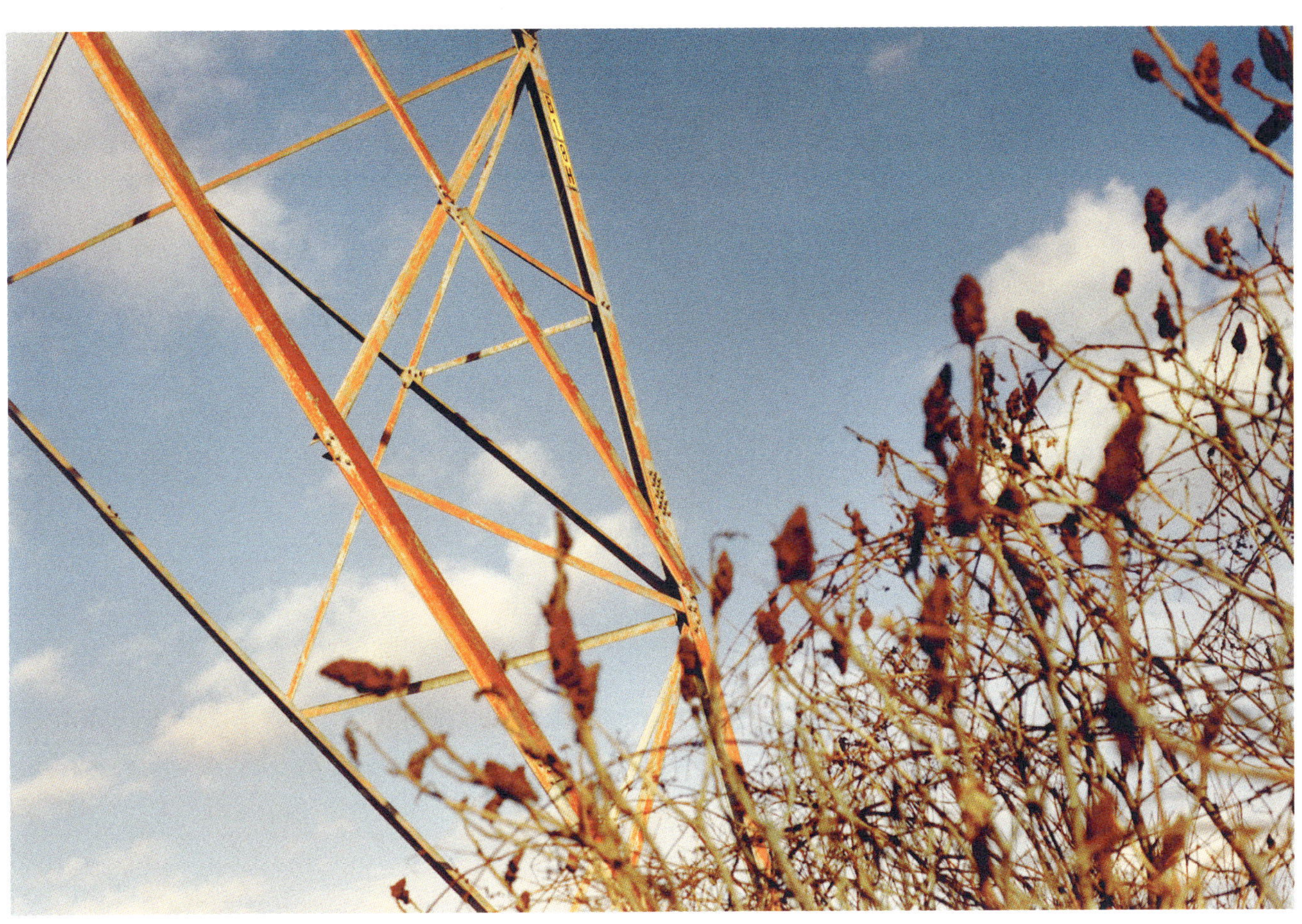

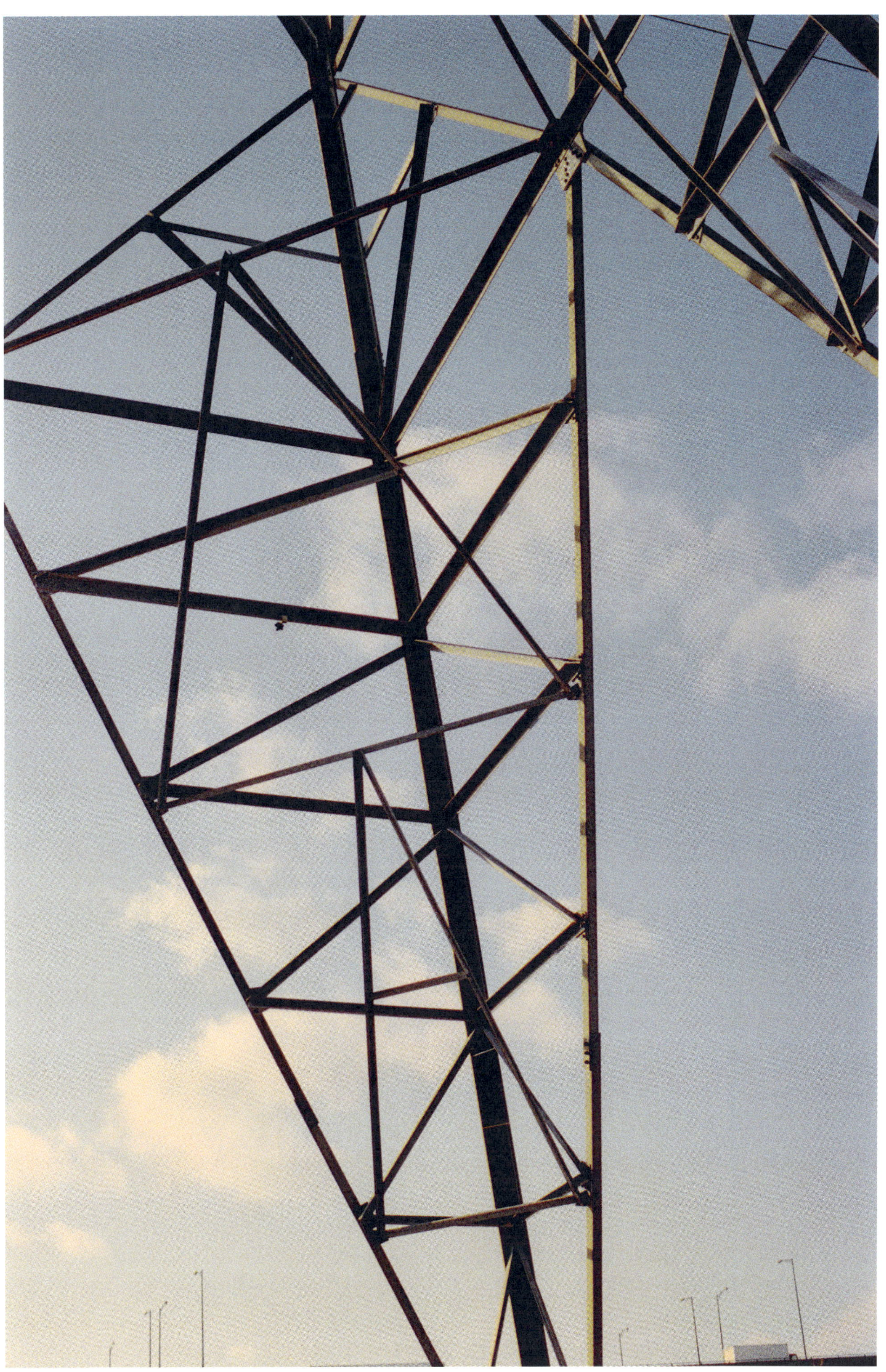

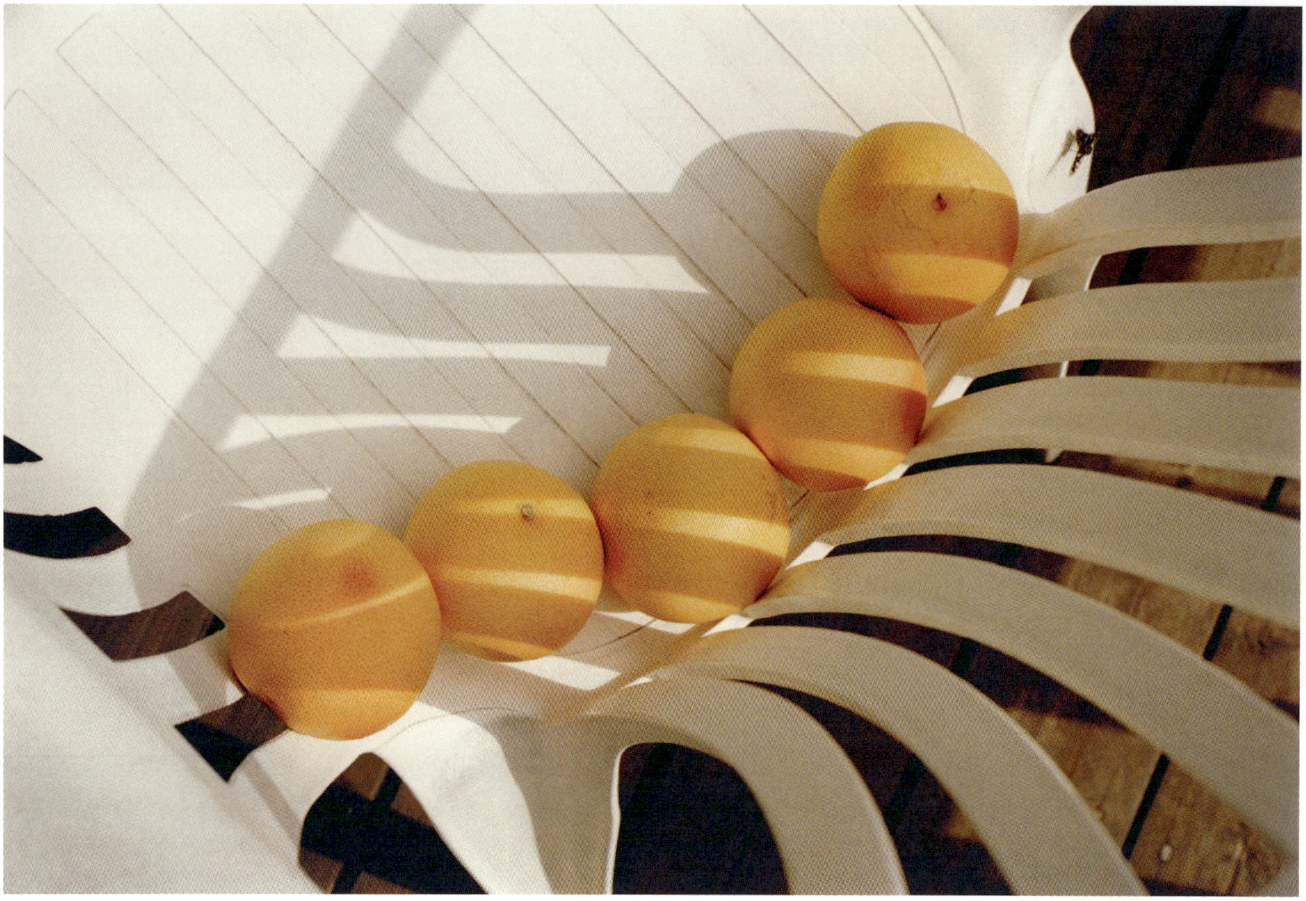

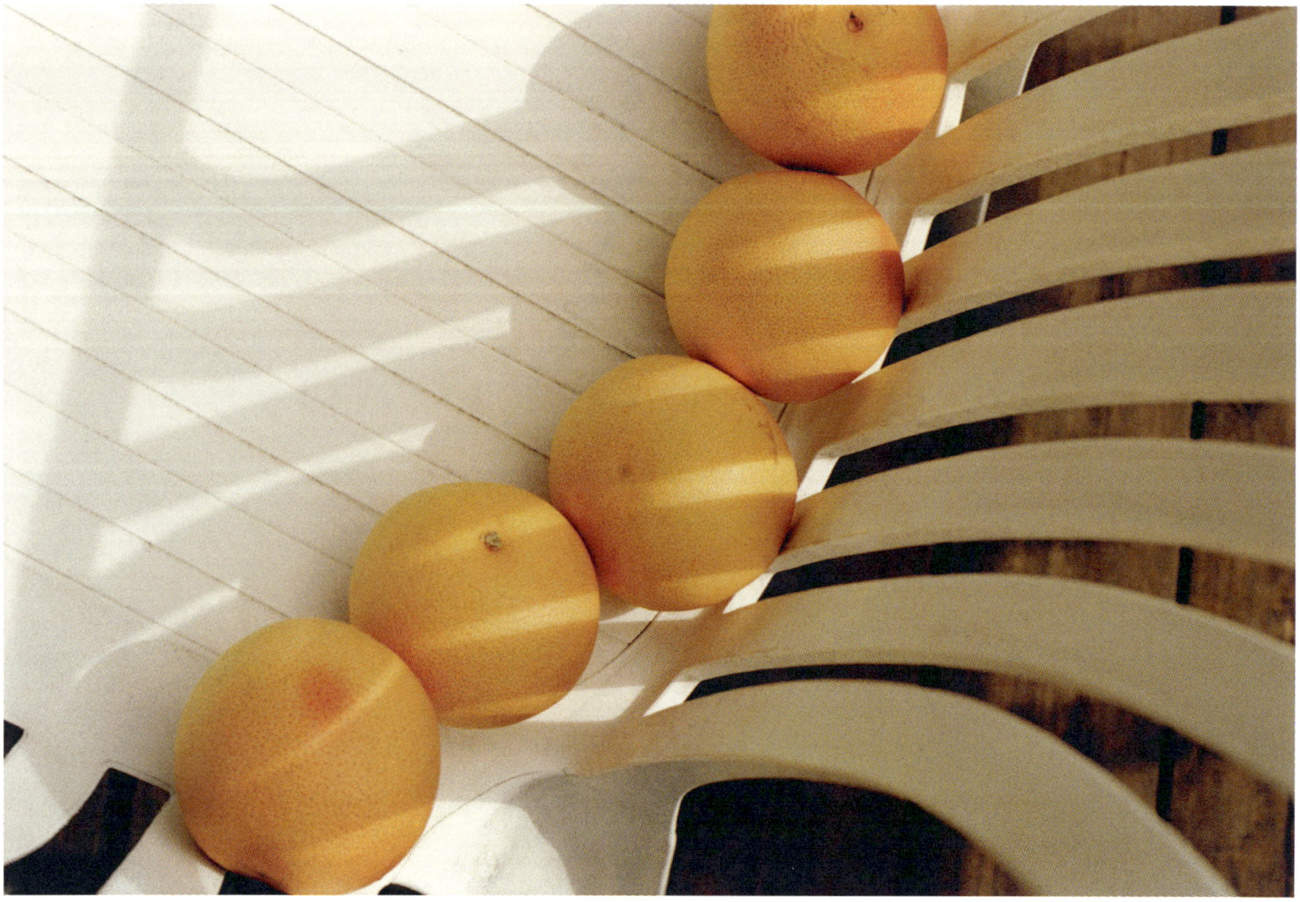

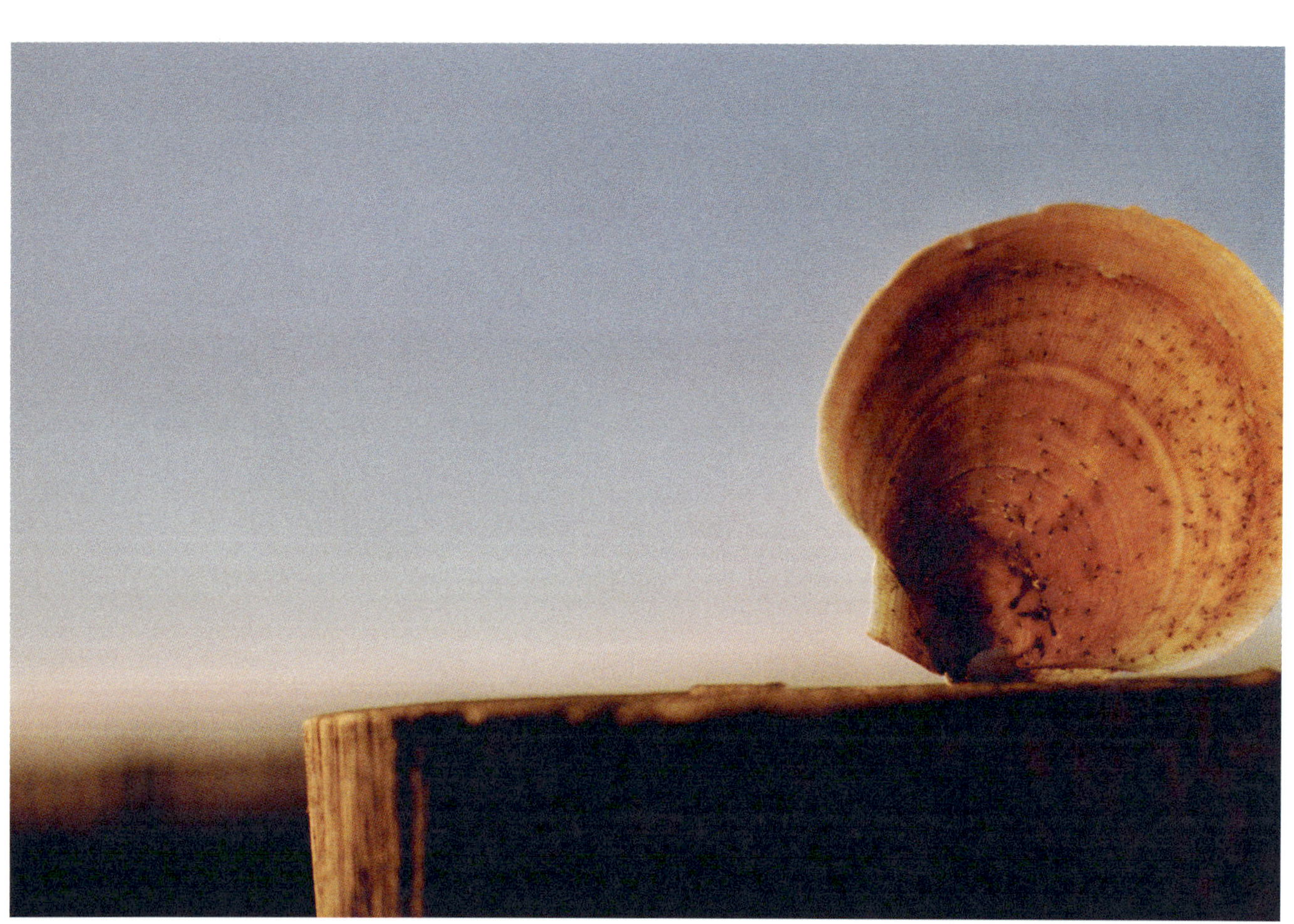

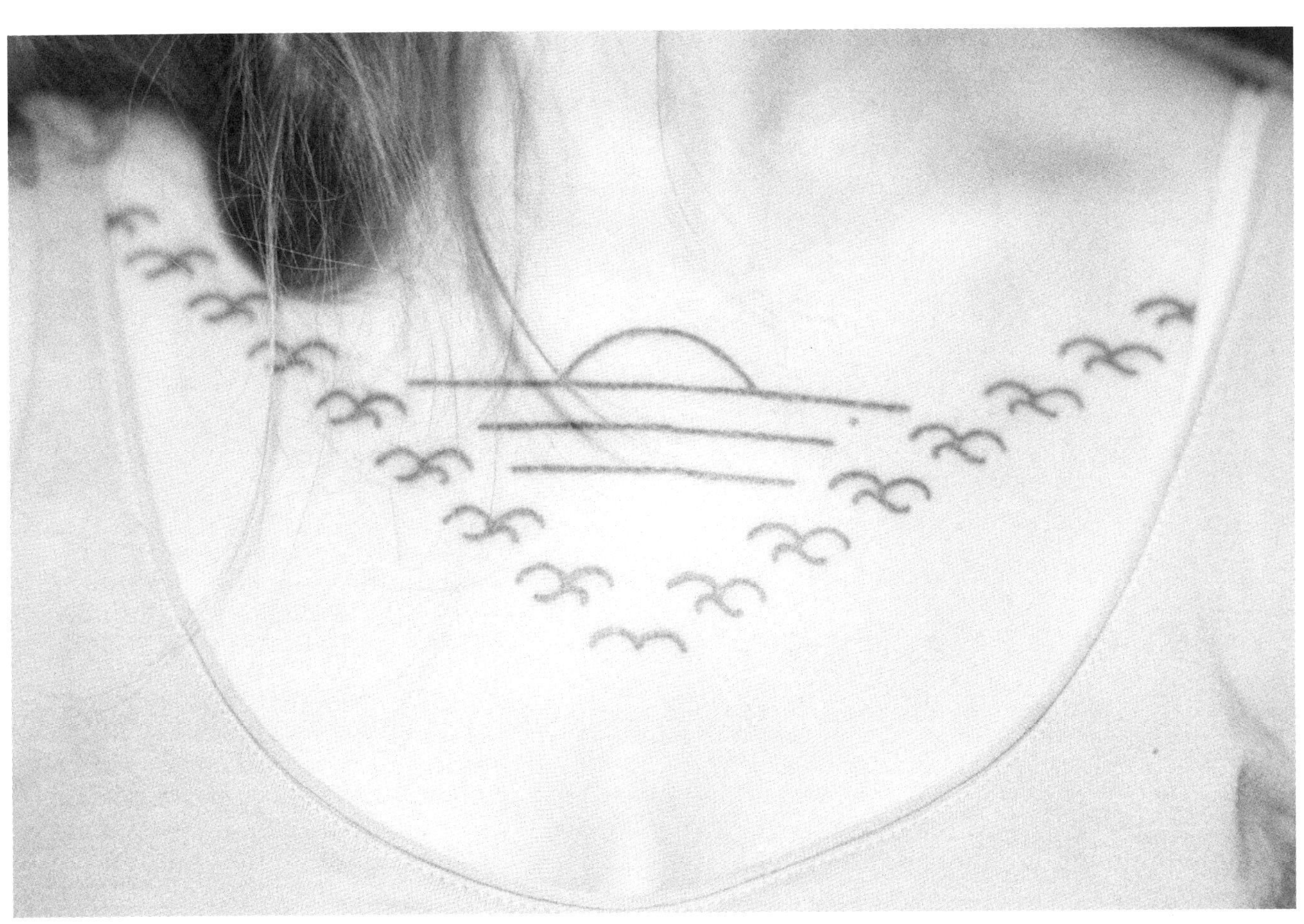

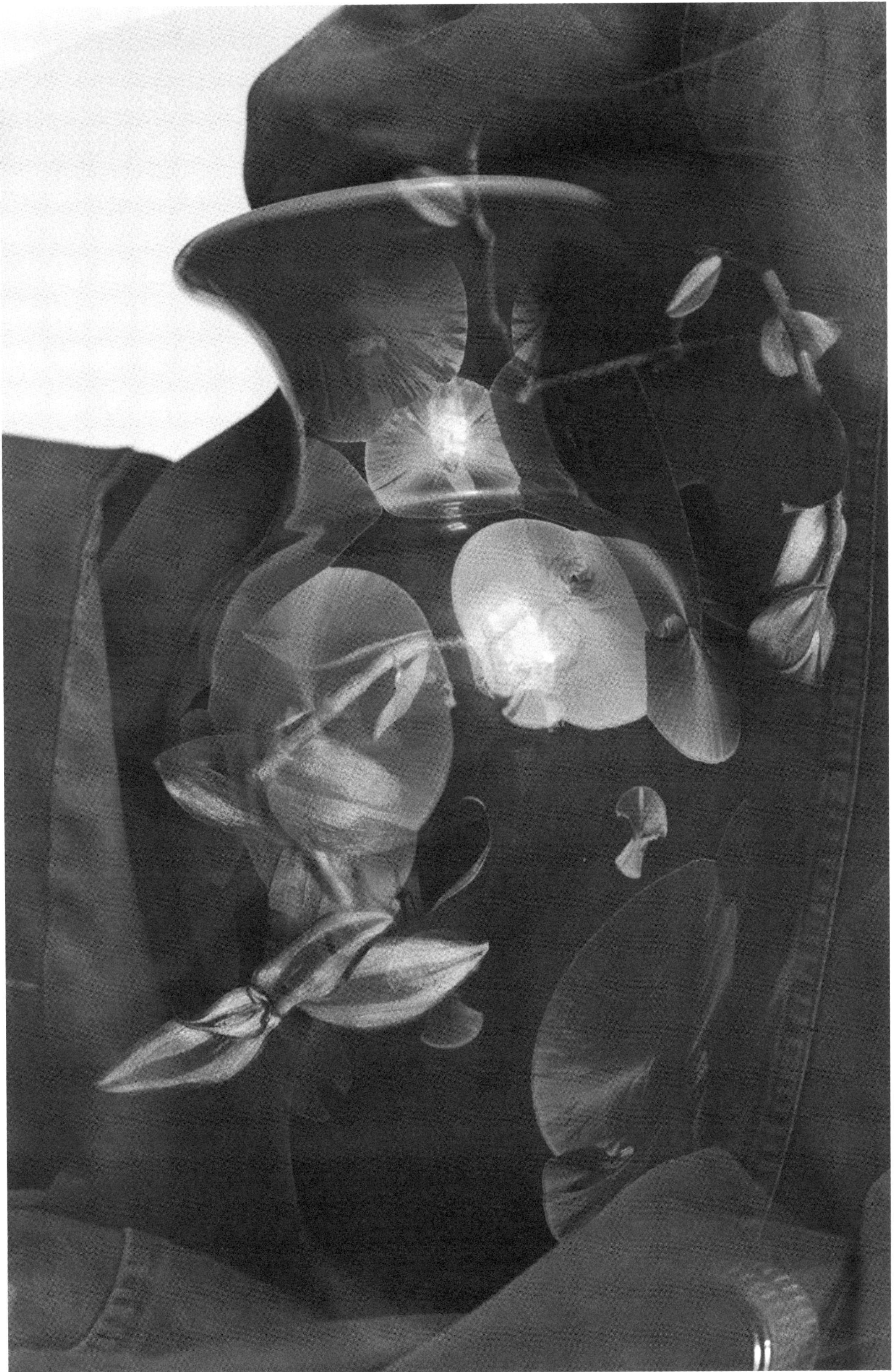

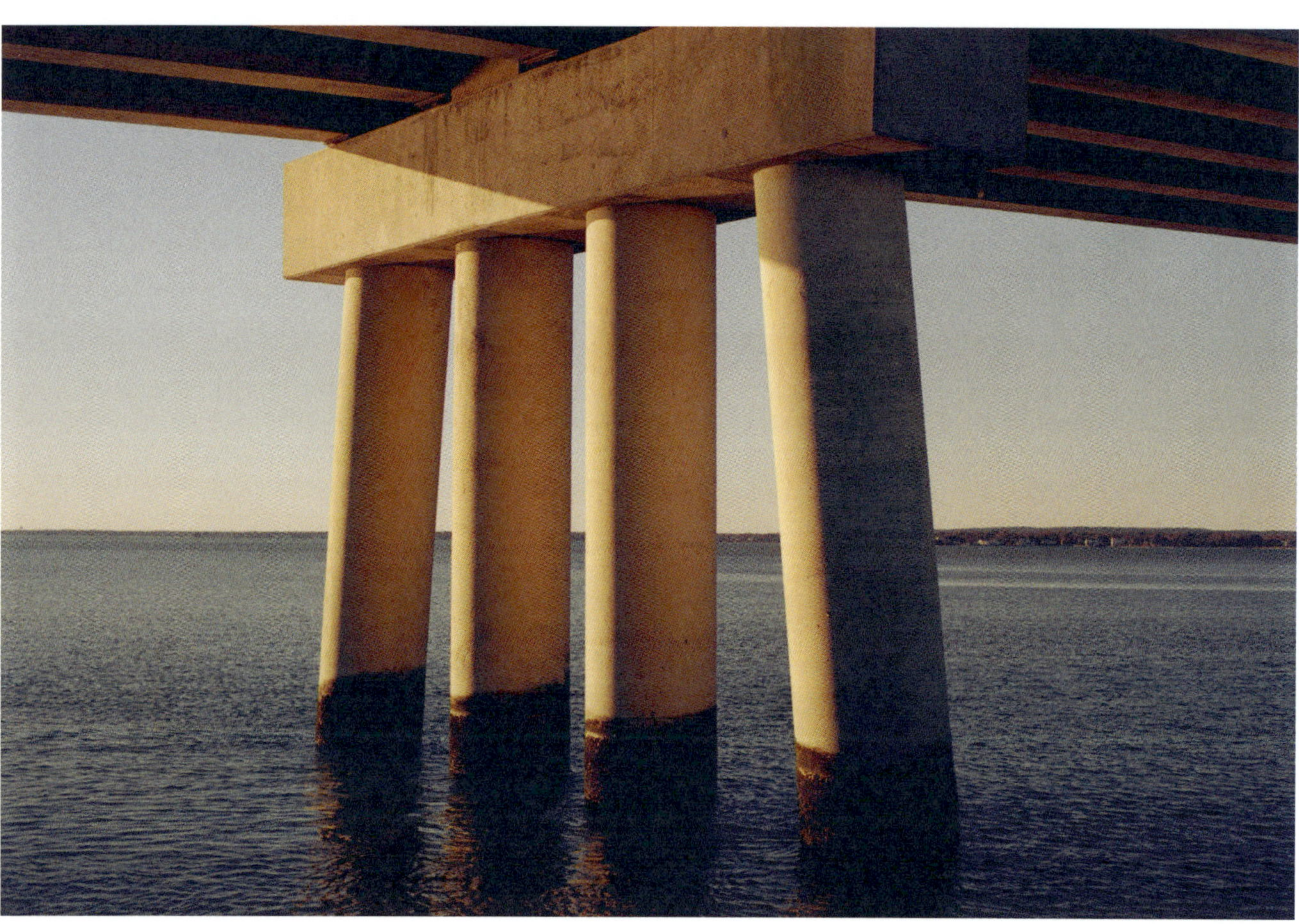

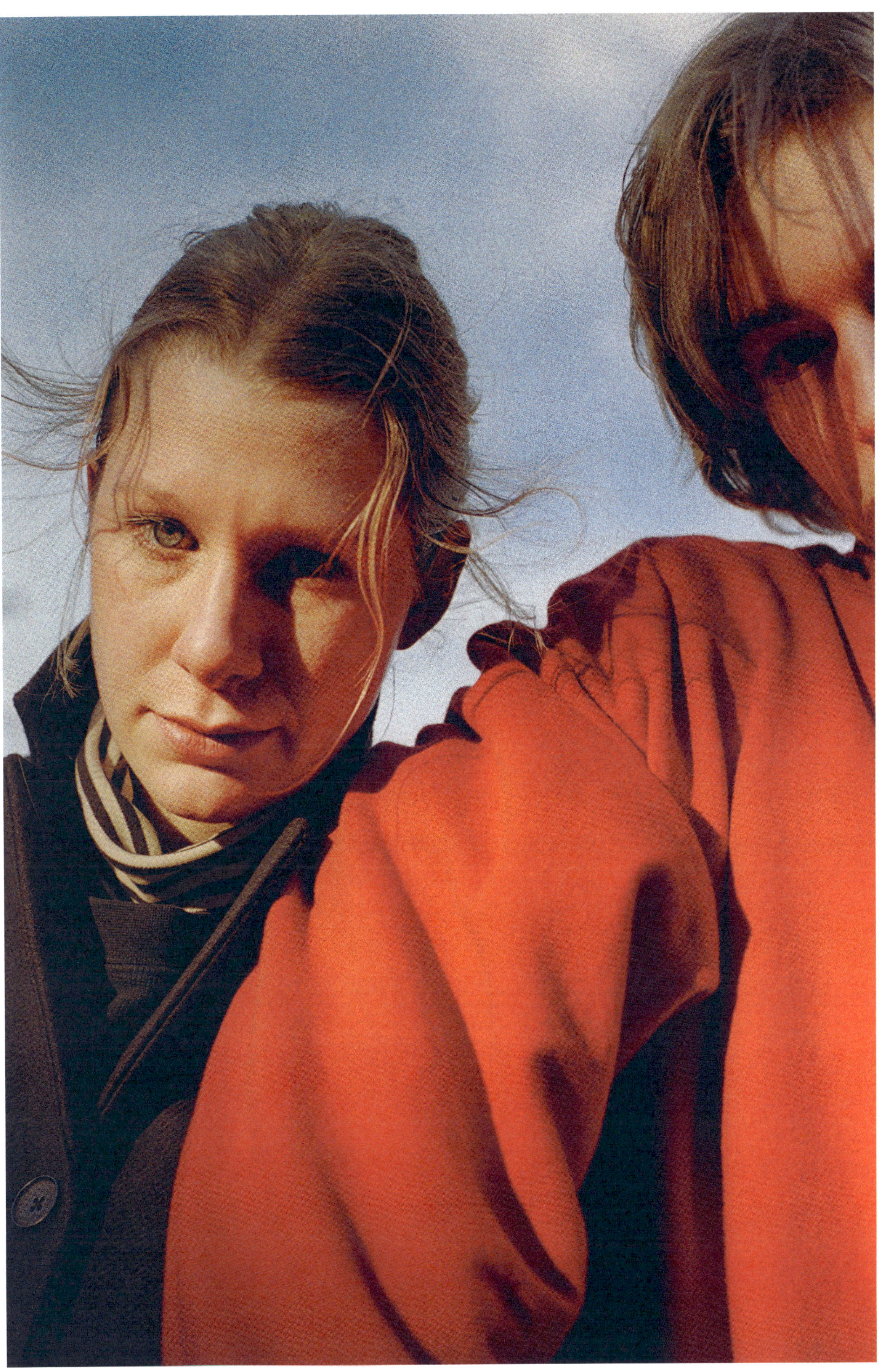

To photograph your reflection in a mirror, the camera's view must be focused to a distance beyond the mirror's surface, doubling the distance from the camera to the mirror.

The camera is focusing into the reflection rather than onto the surface reflecting the present image. This basic technical information suggests the distance and obstructions between photographer and subject.

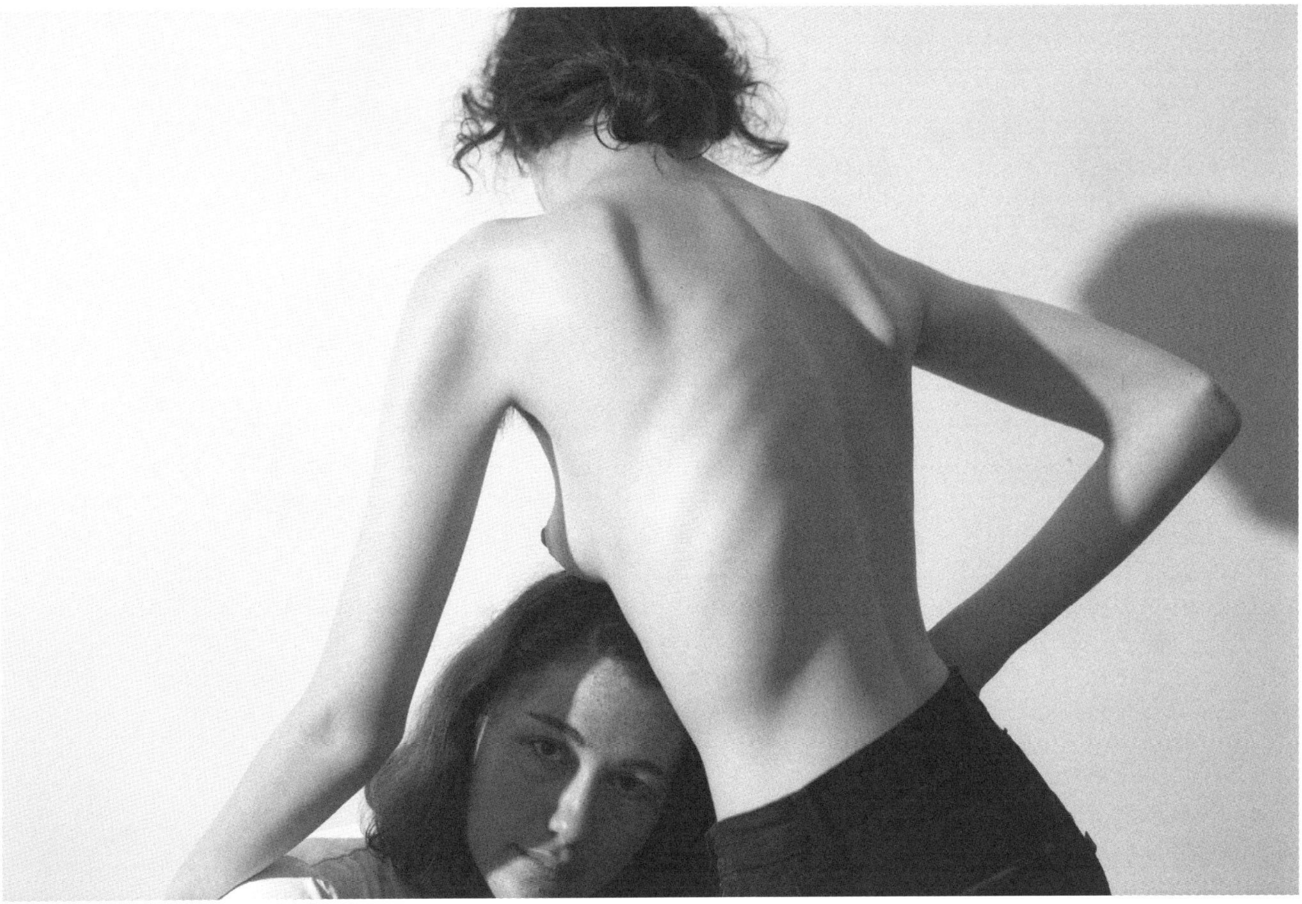

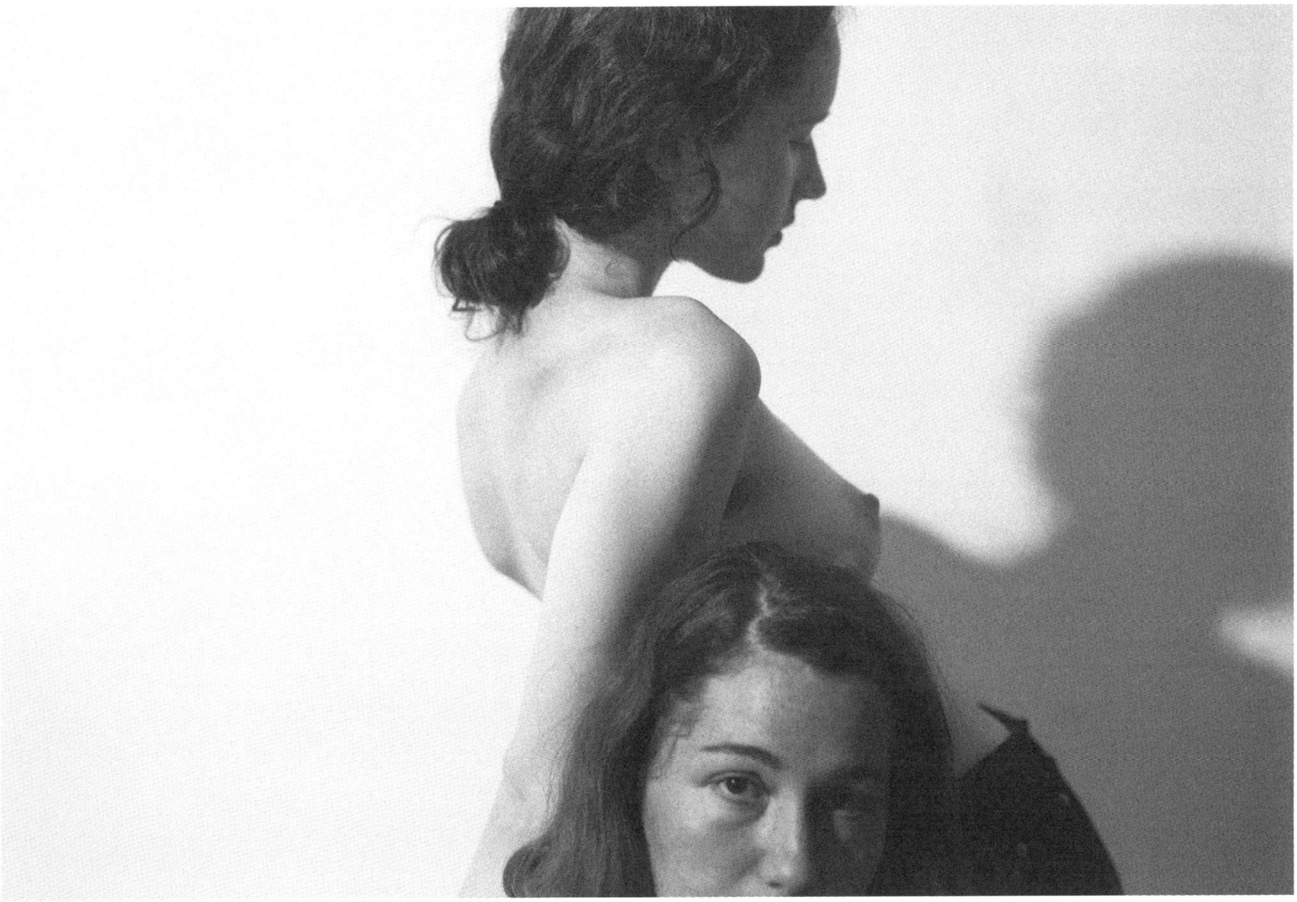

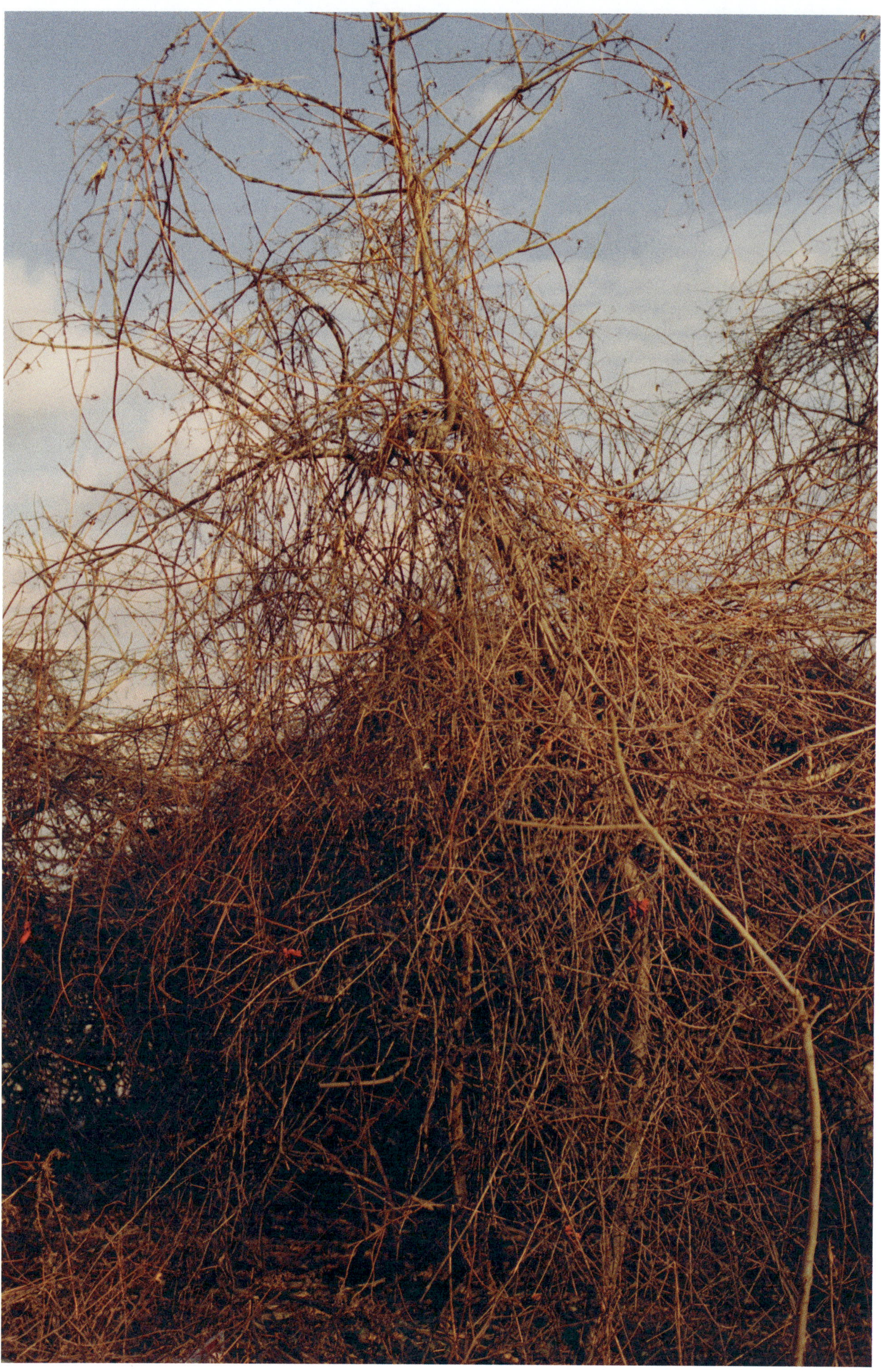

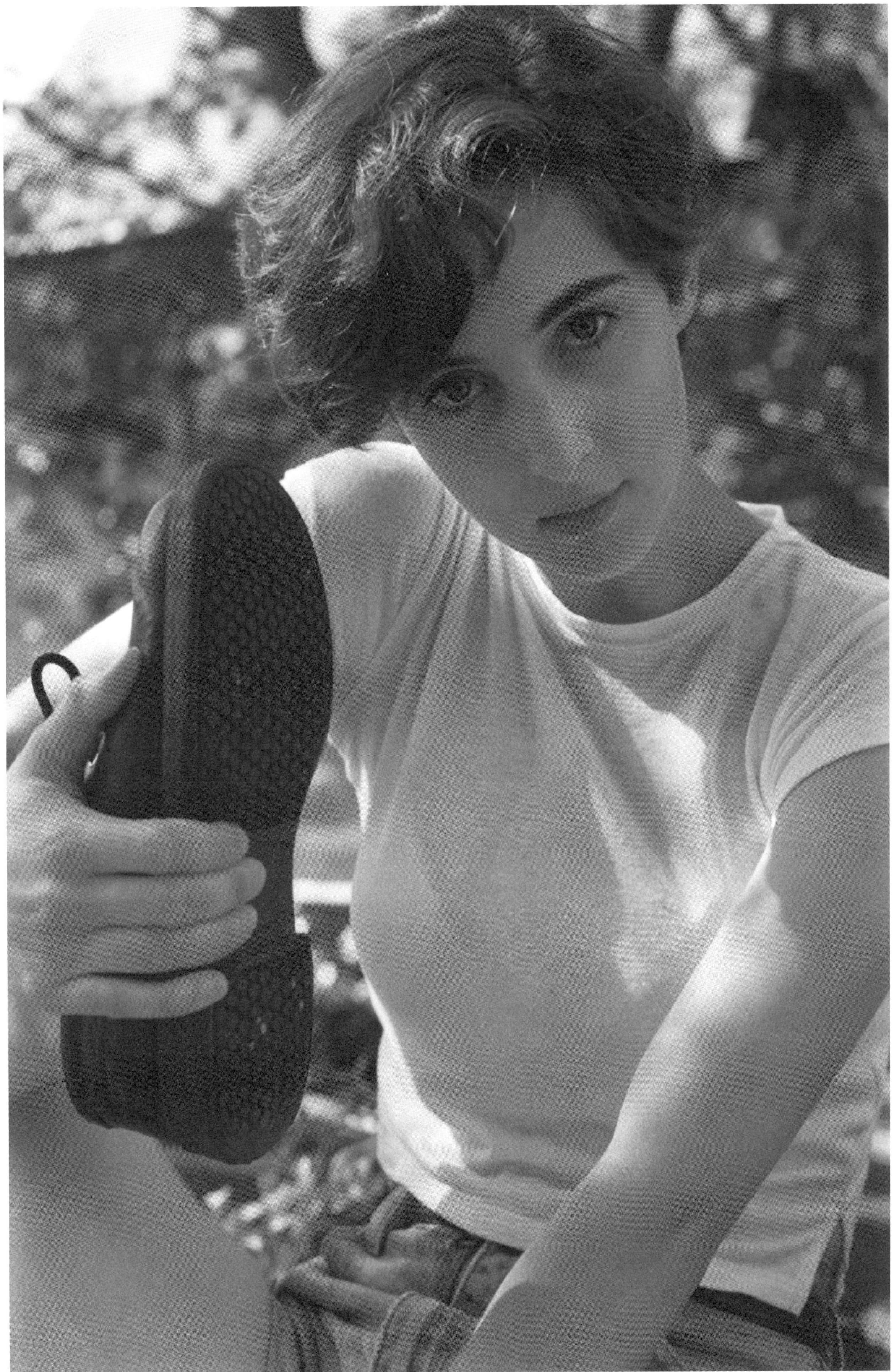

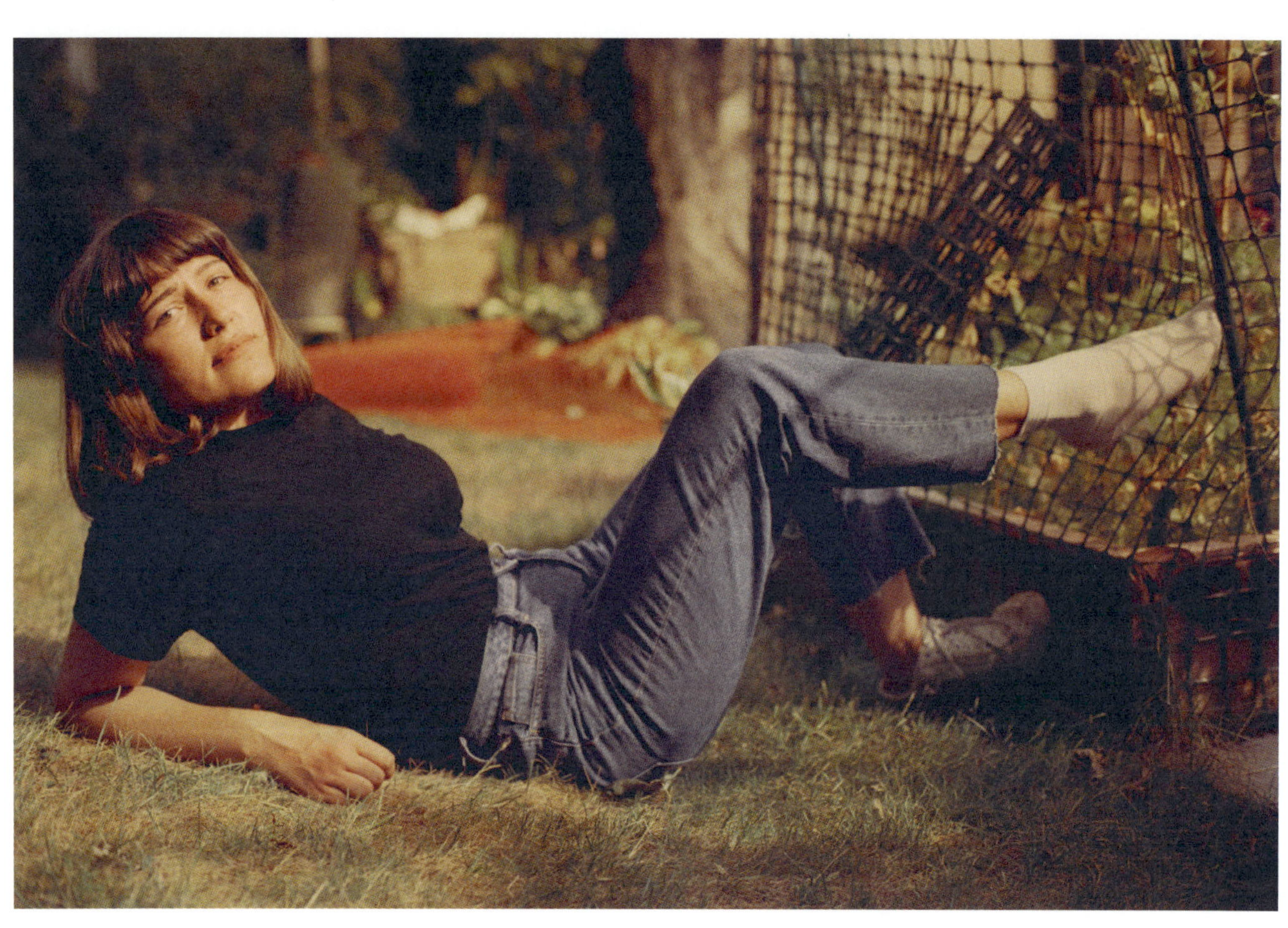

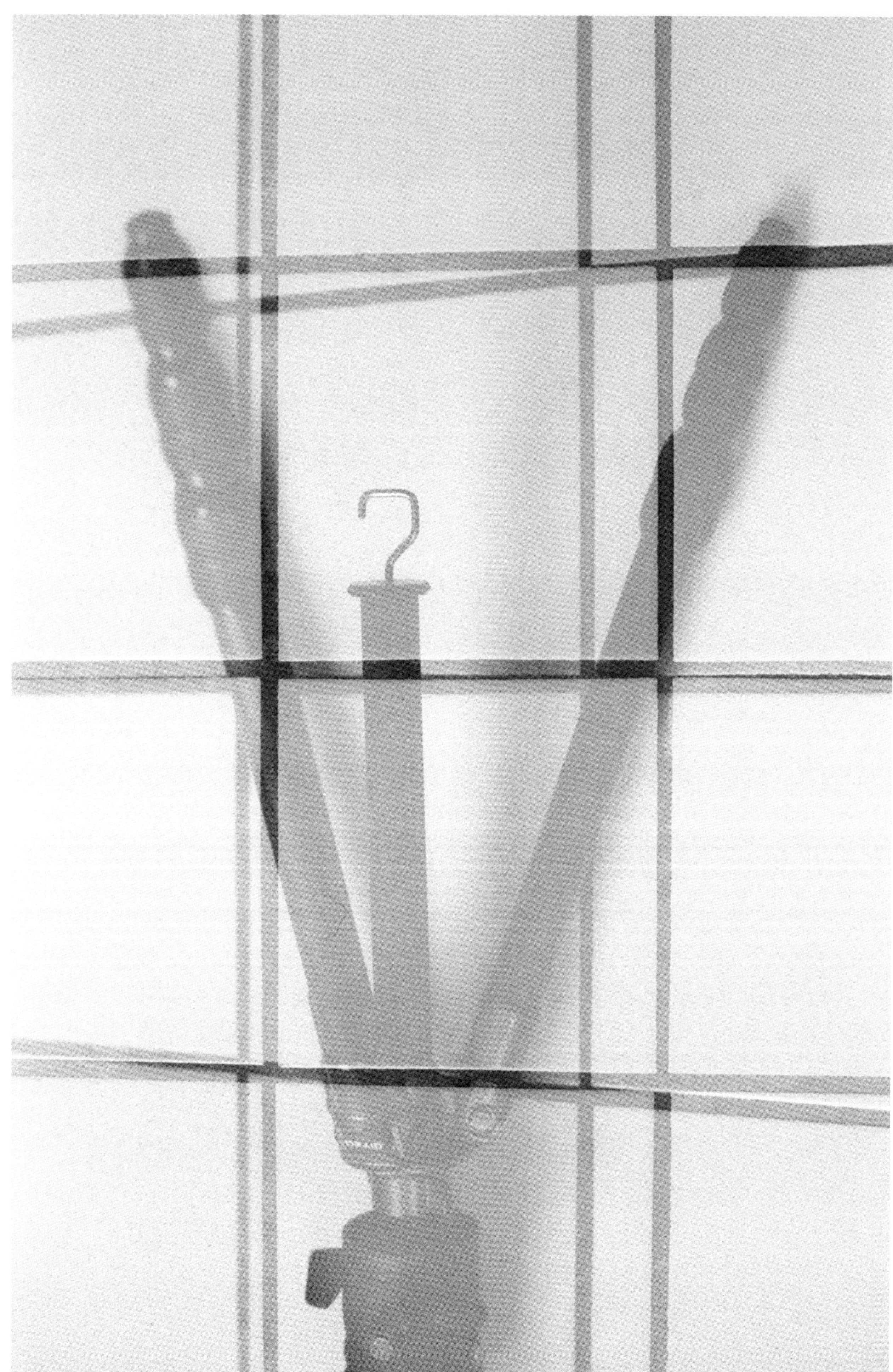

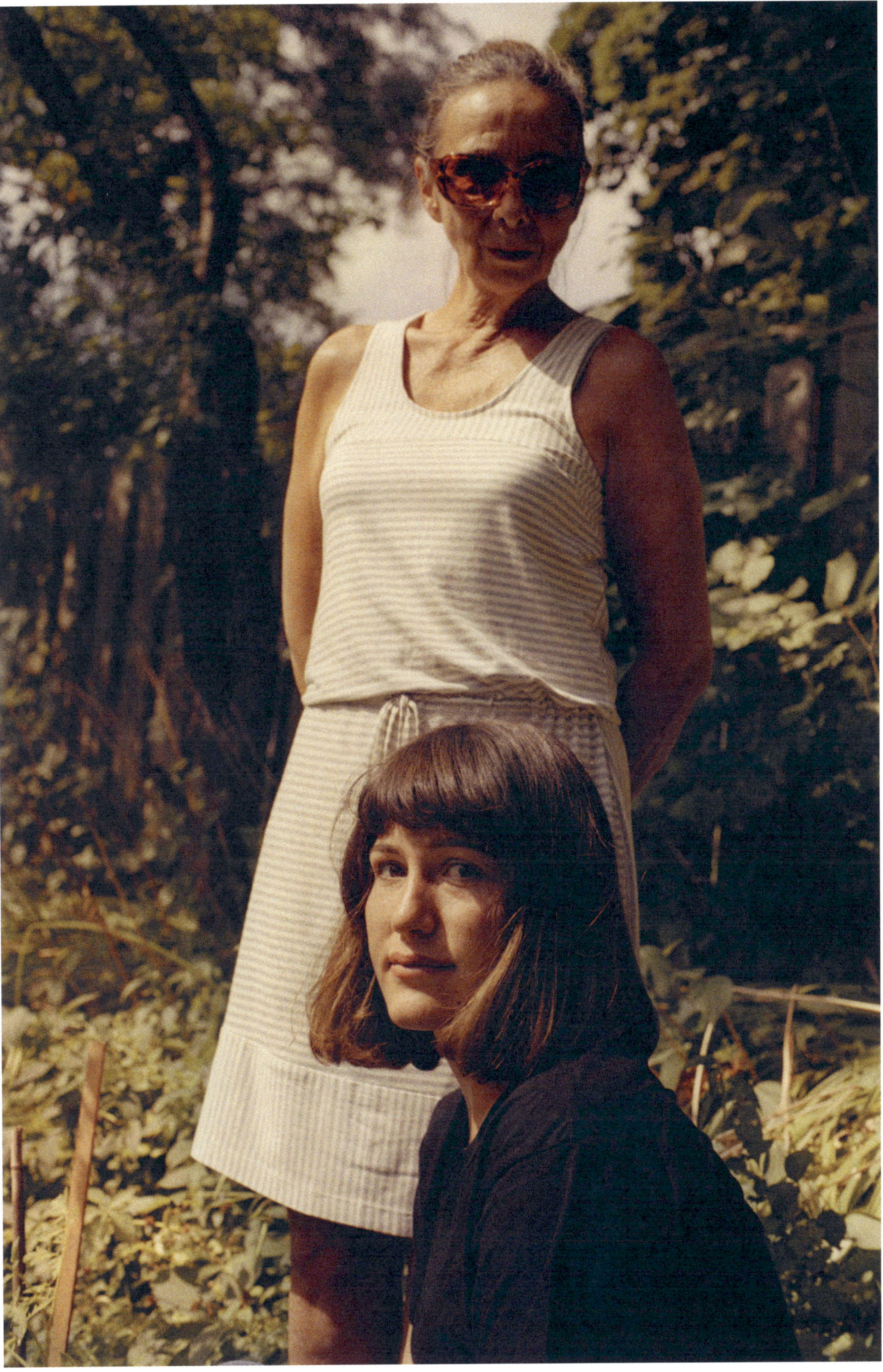

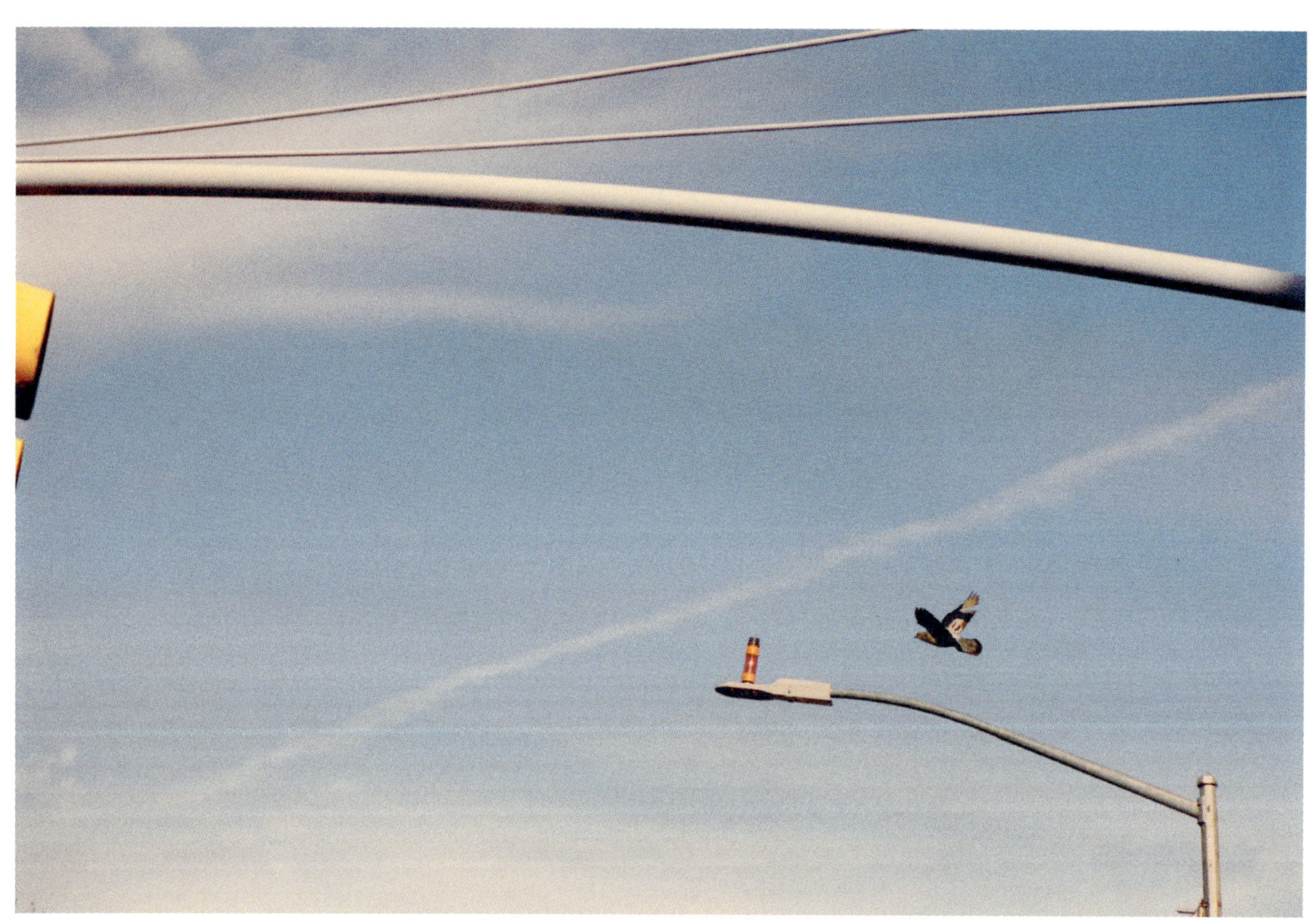

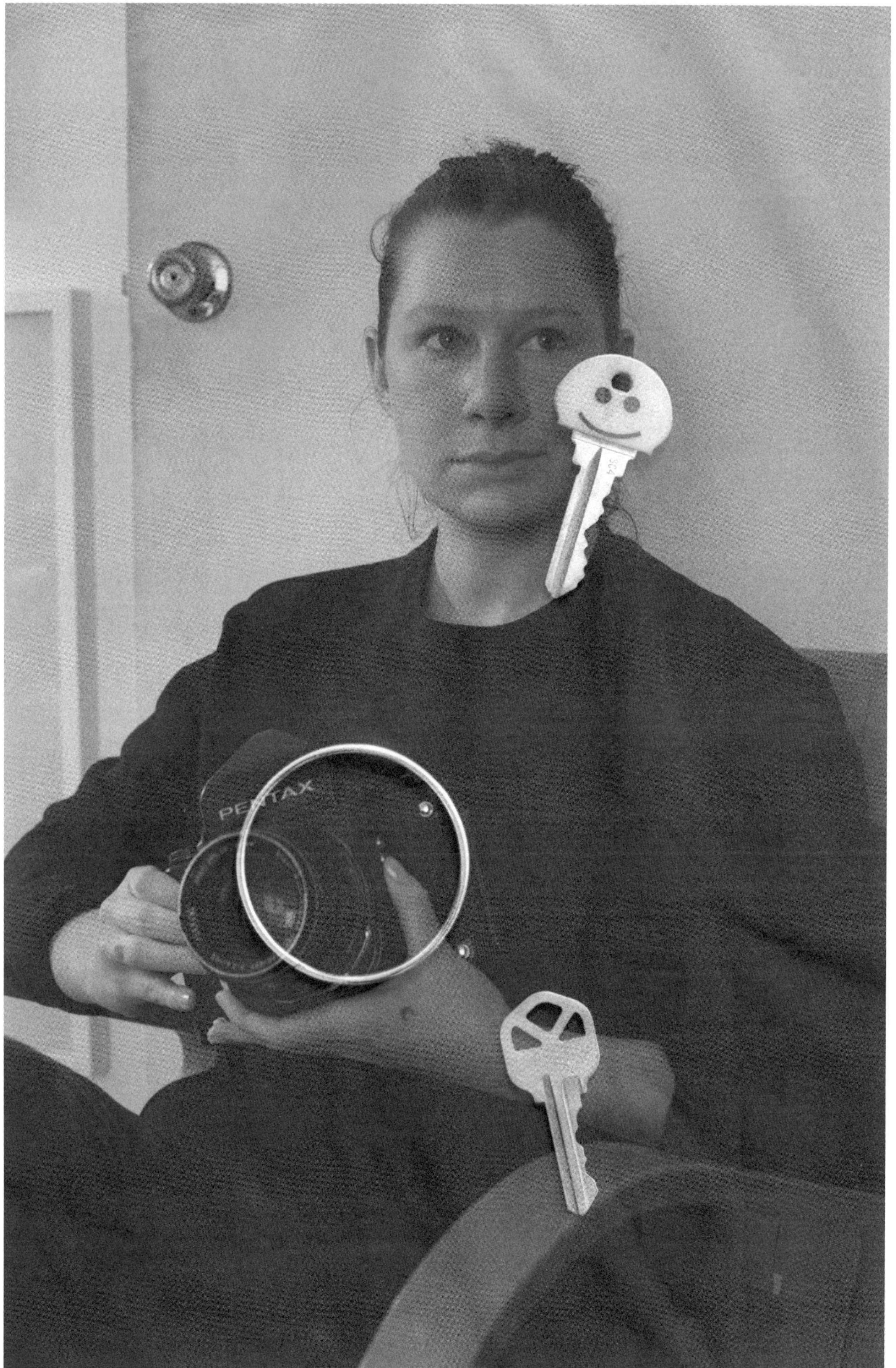

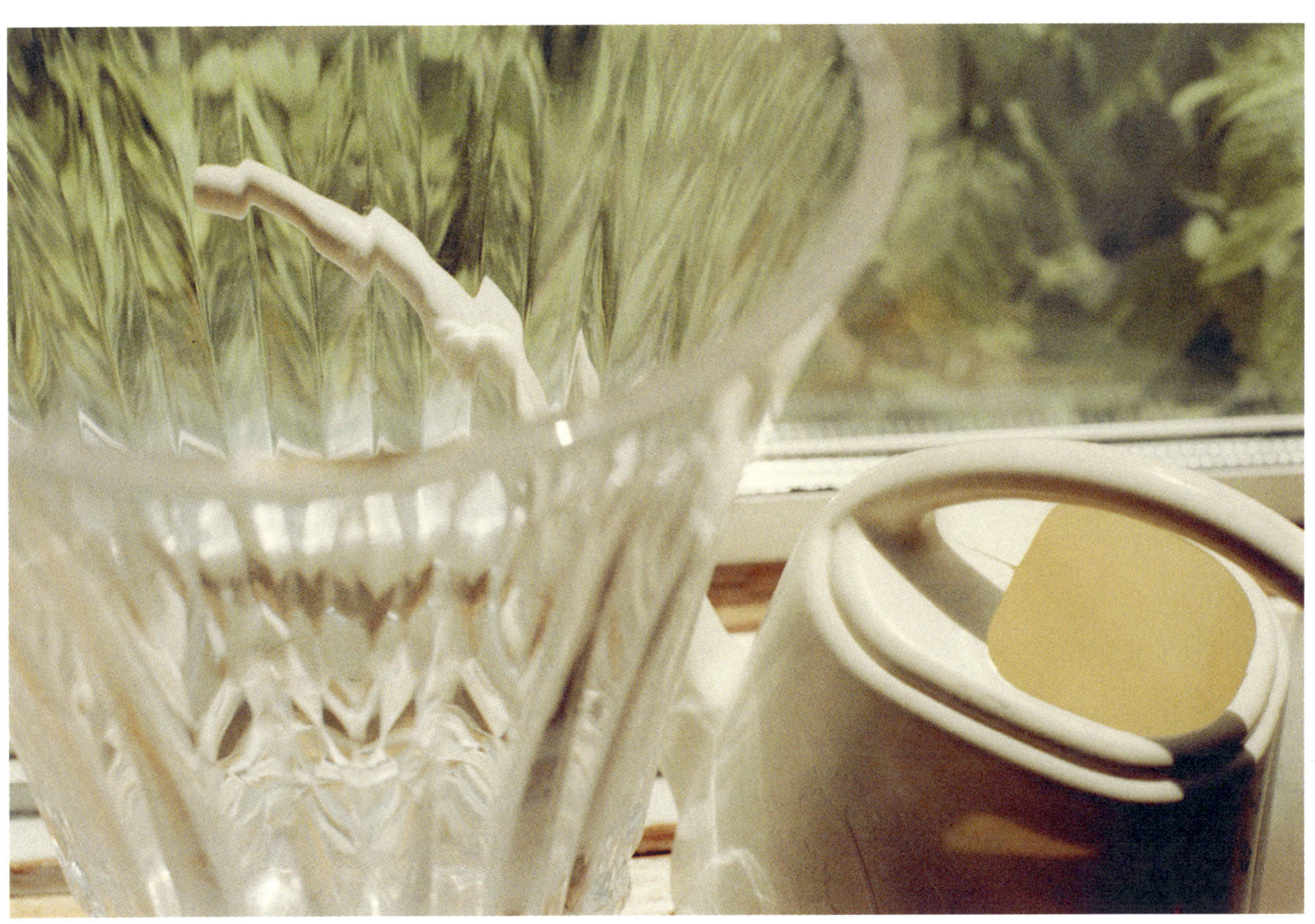

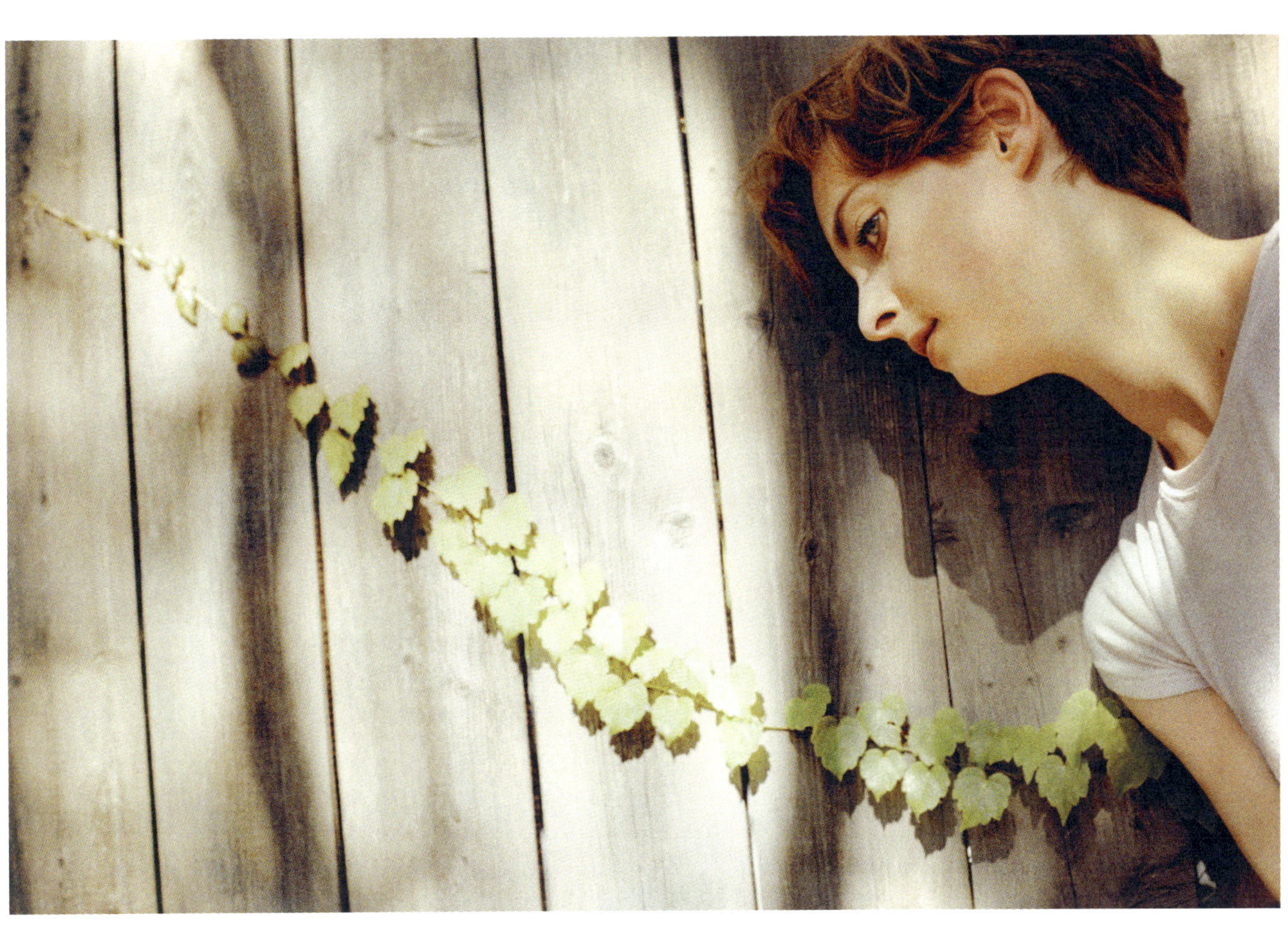

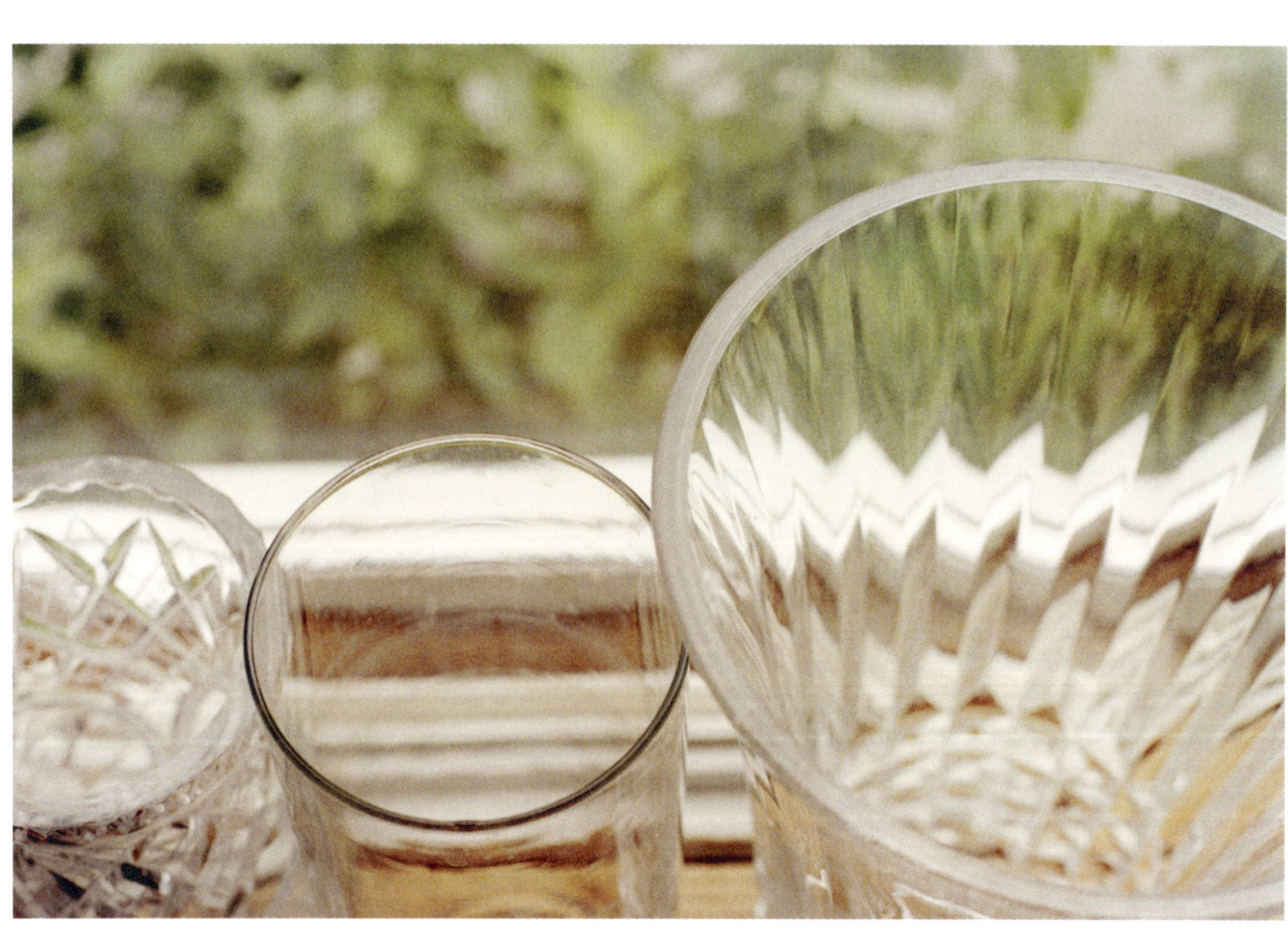

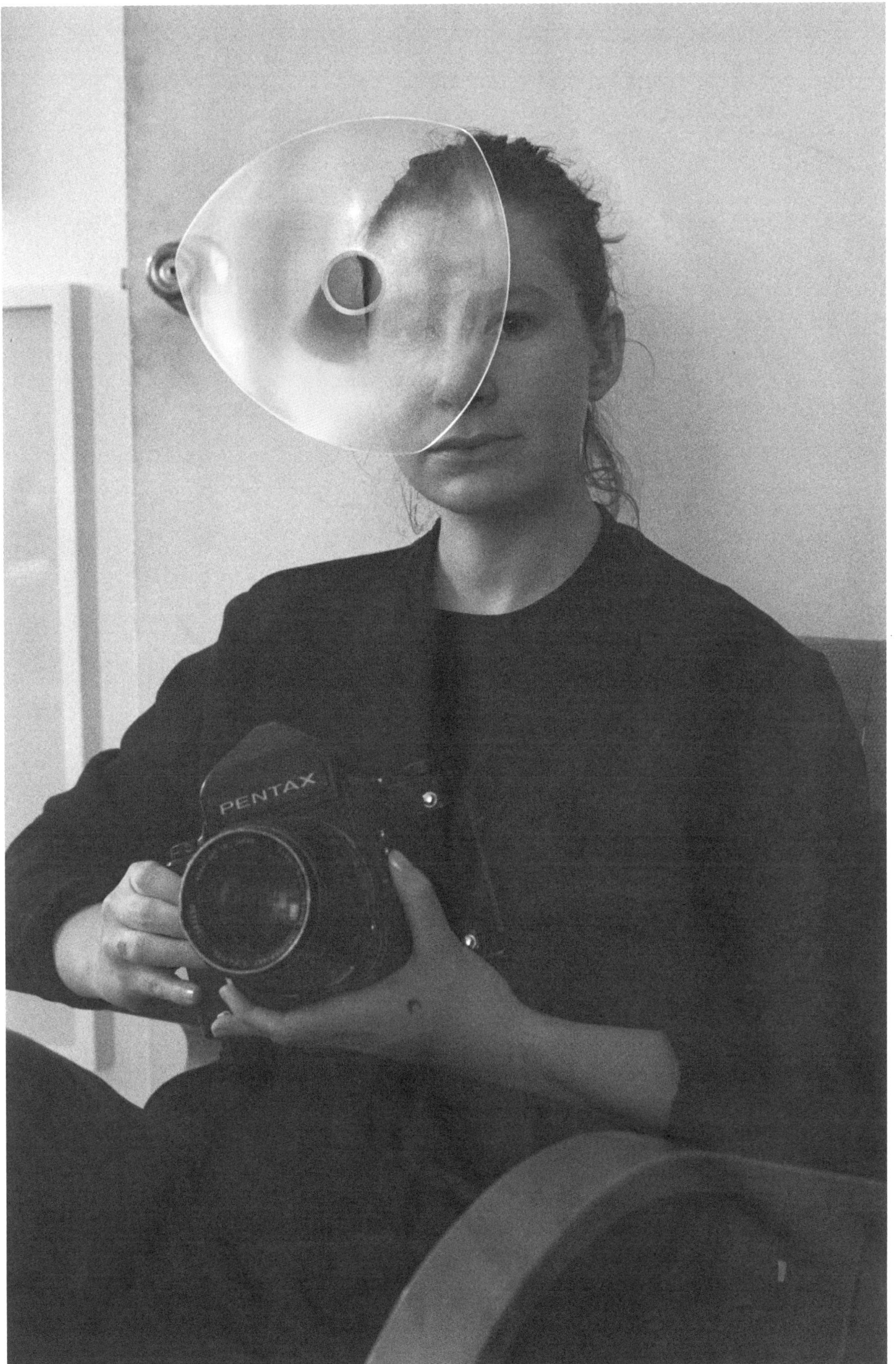

In a brief daybook entry, Edward Weston famously mused on the idea of form following function.

'October 21, 1949 - "Form follows Function". Who said this I don't know, but the writer spoke well.'

When Weston isolated the form in his photographic compositions, he pointed, firstly, to the inherent histories and movements within the function of his subjects' forms. A plant has overheard many conversations during it's growth, a smokestack was designed in response to great technological advancement, and a body is the mark of a life lived.

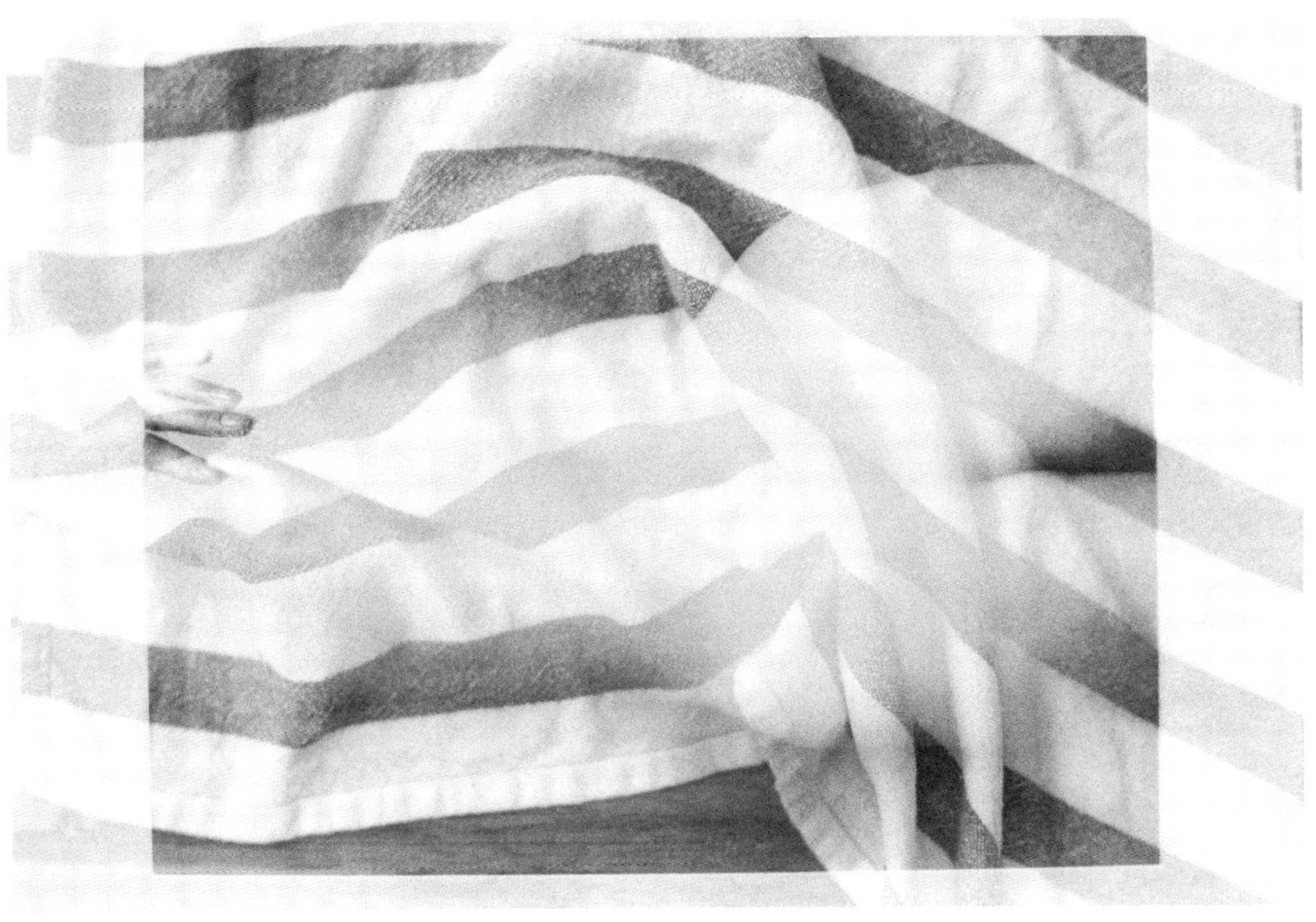

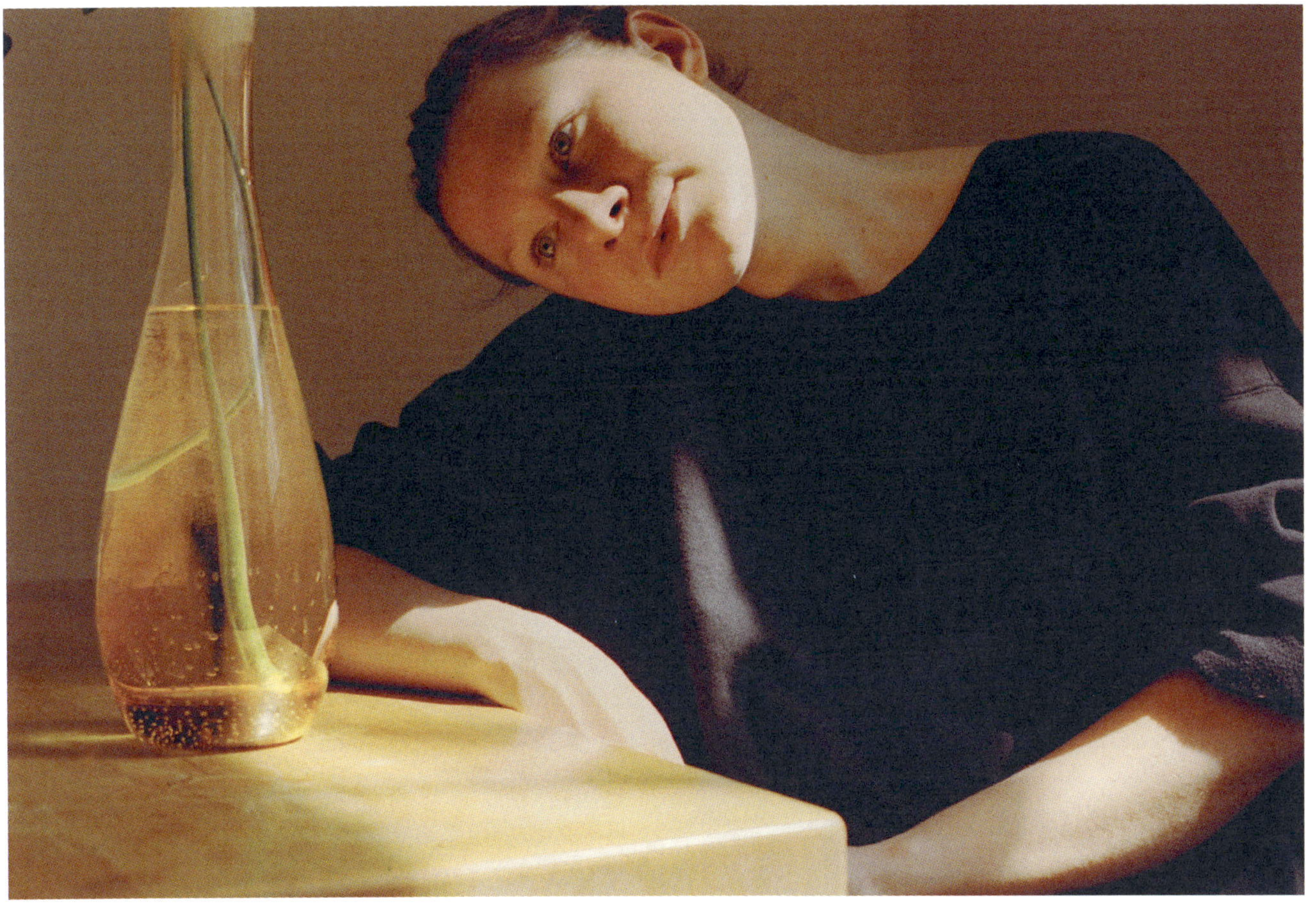

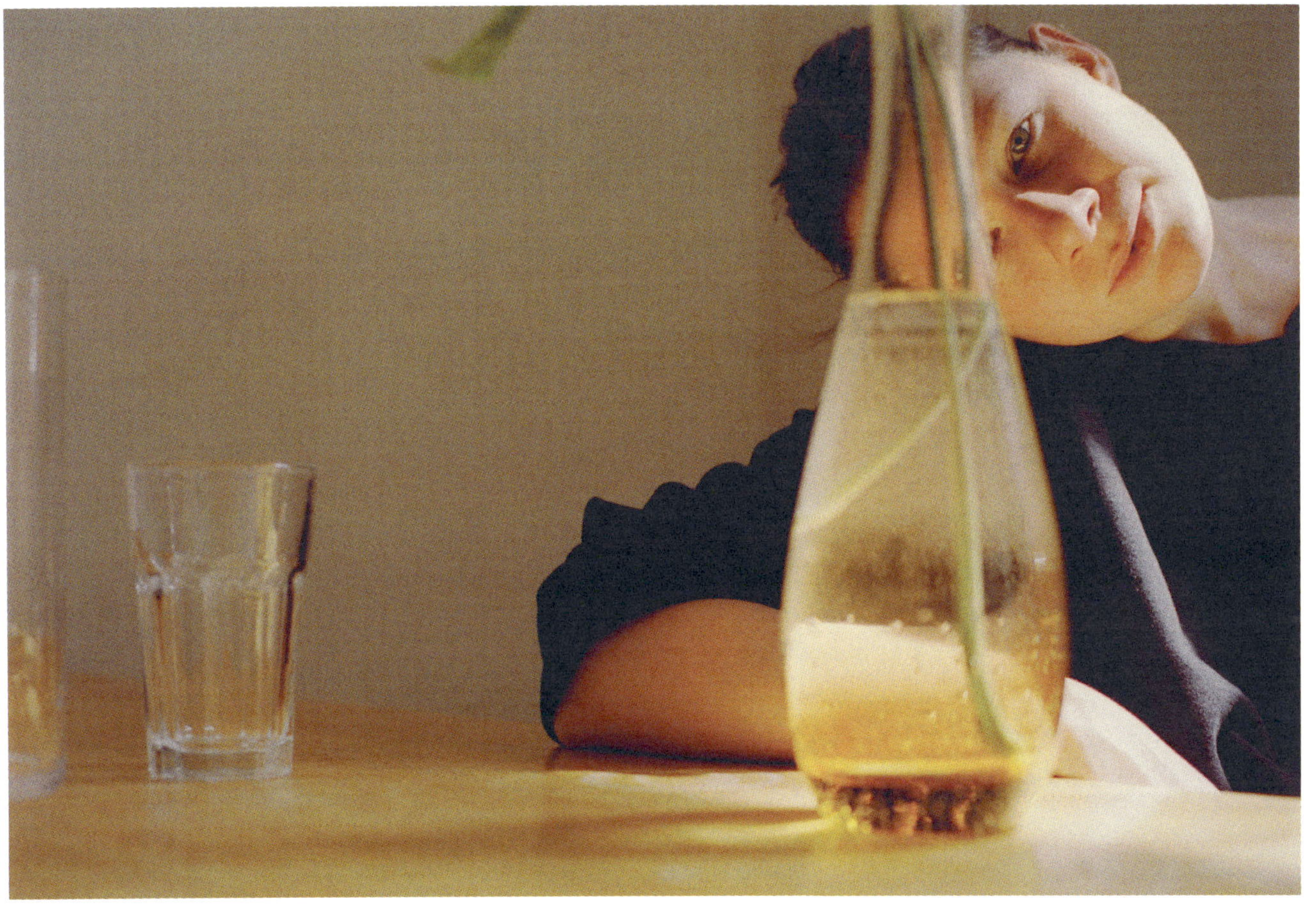

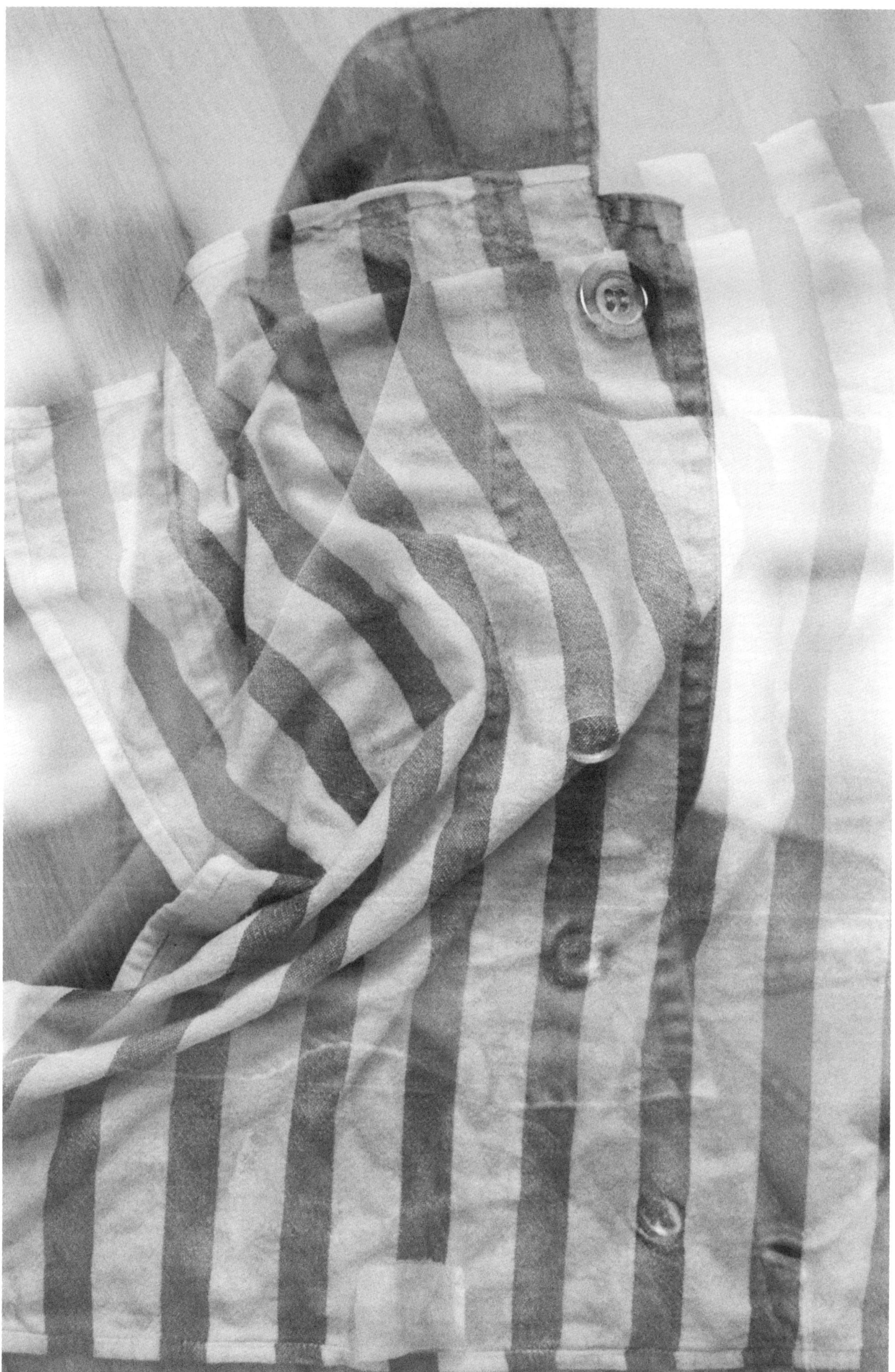

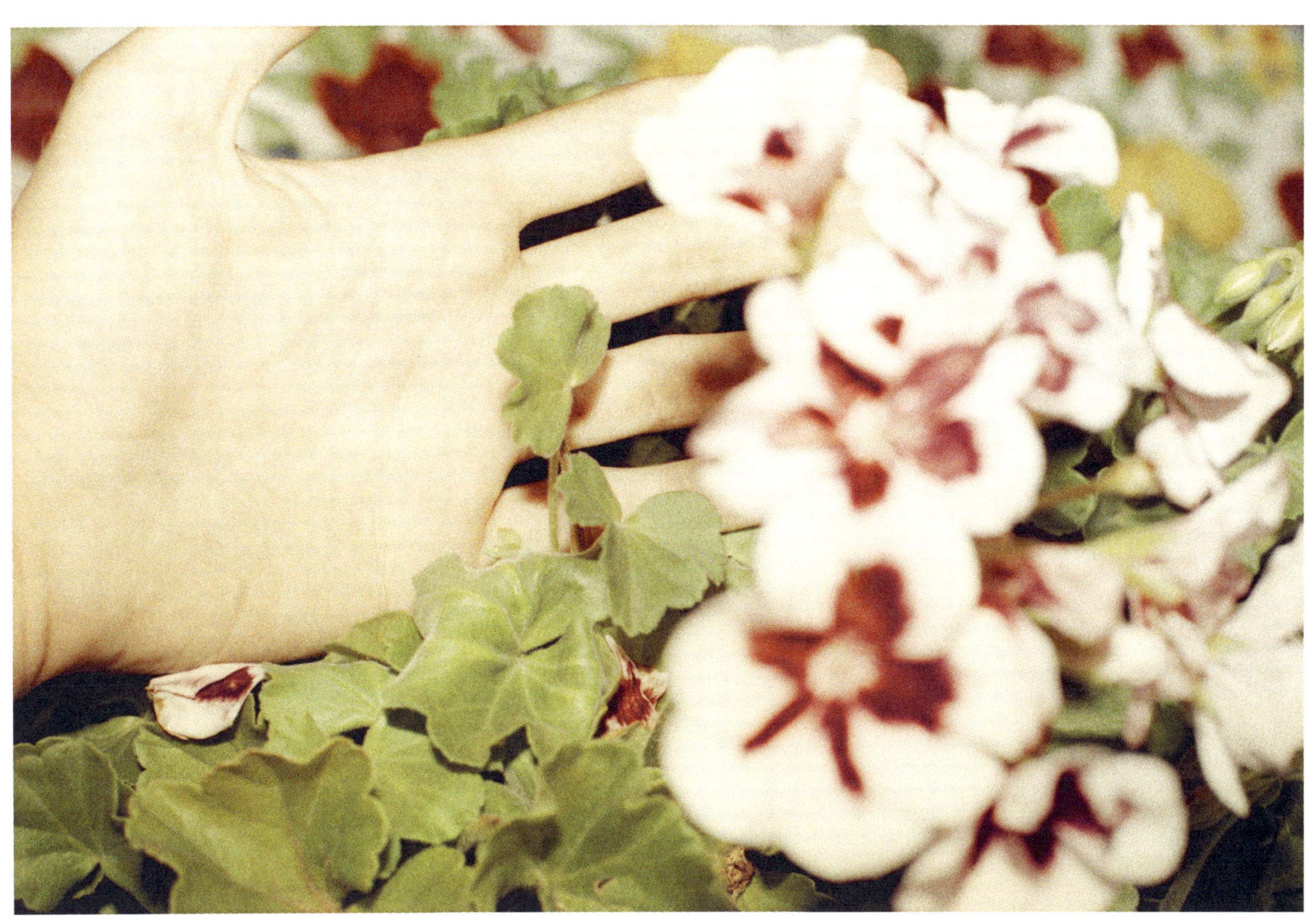

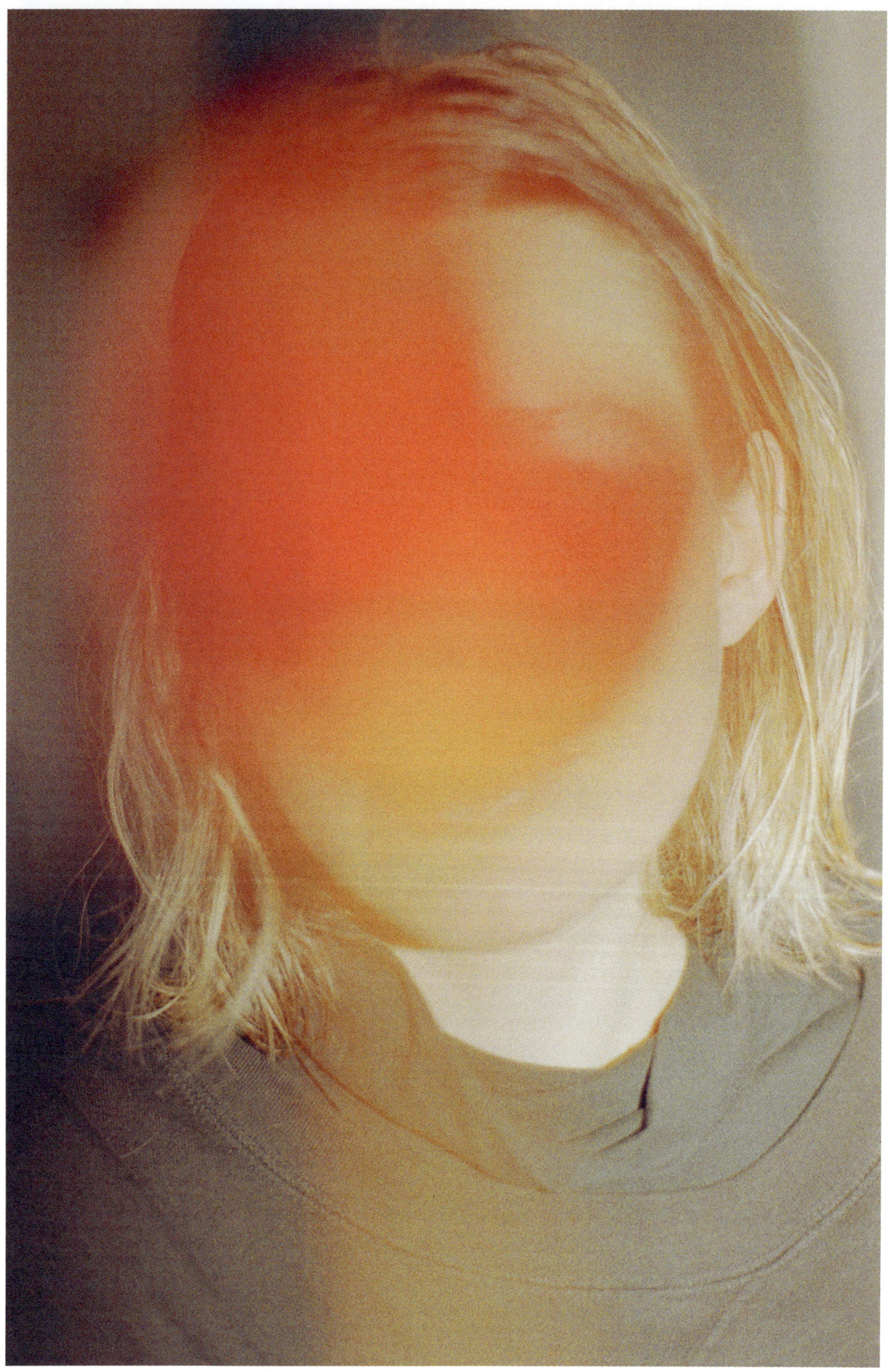

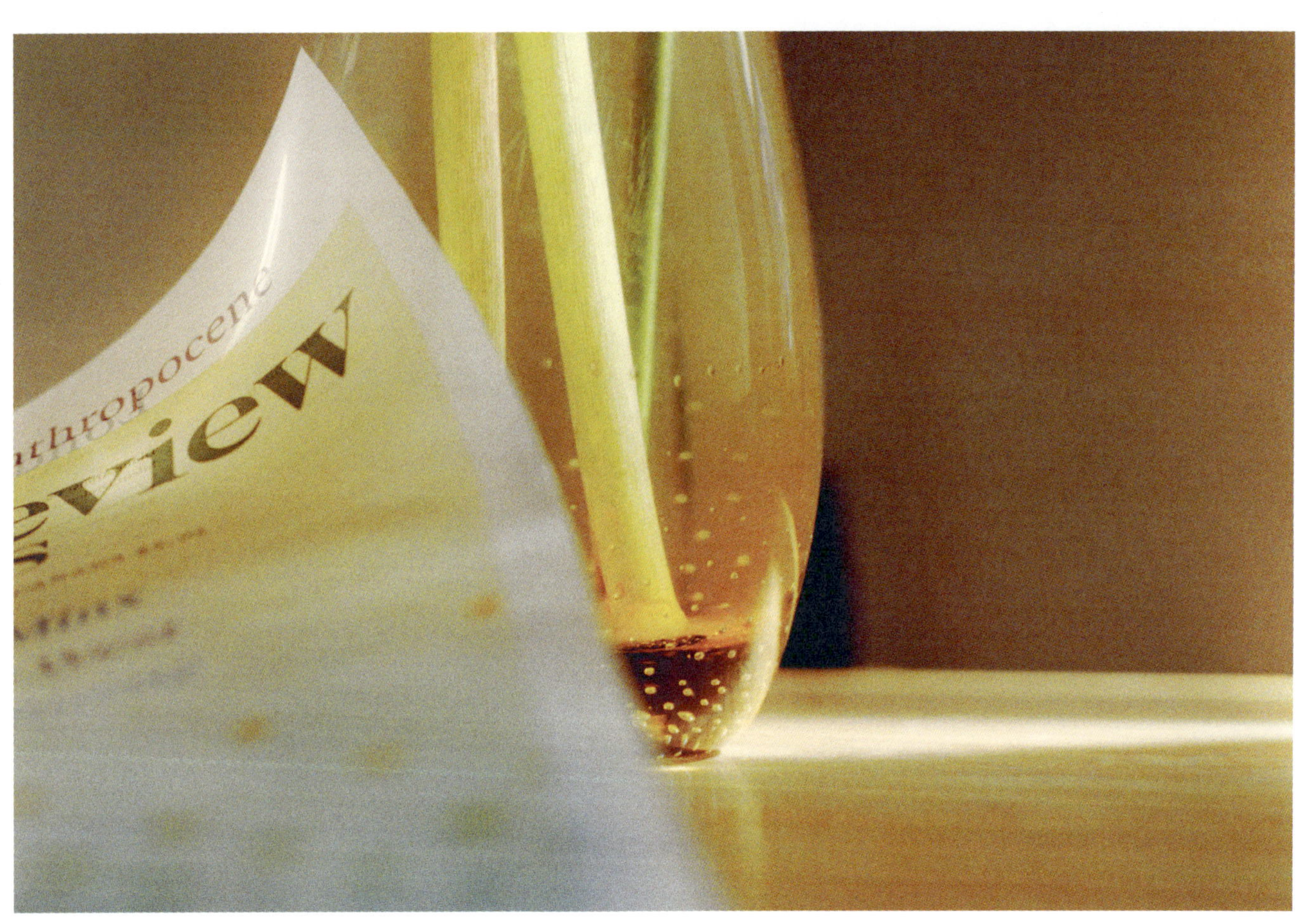
nthropocene
eview

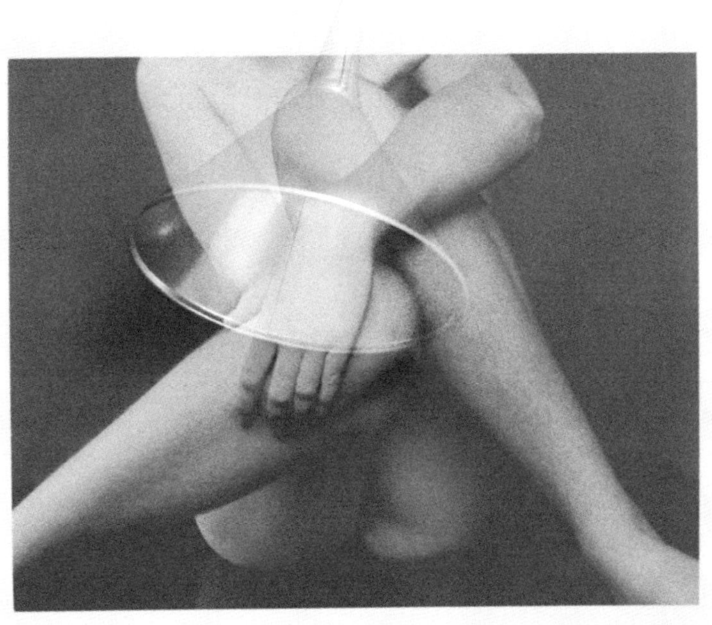

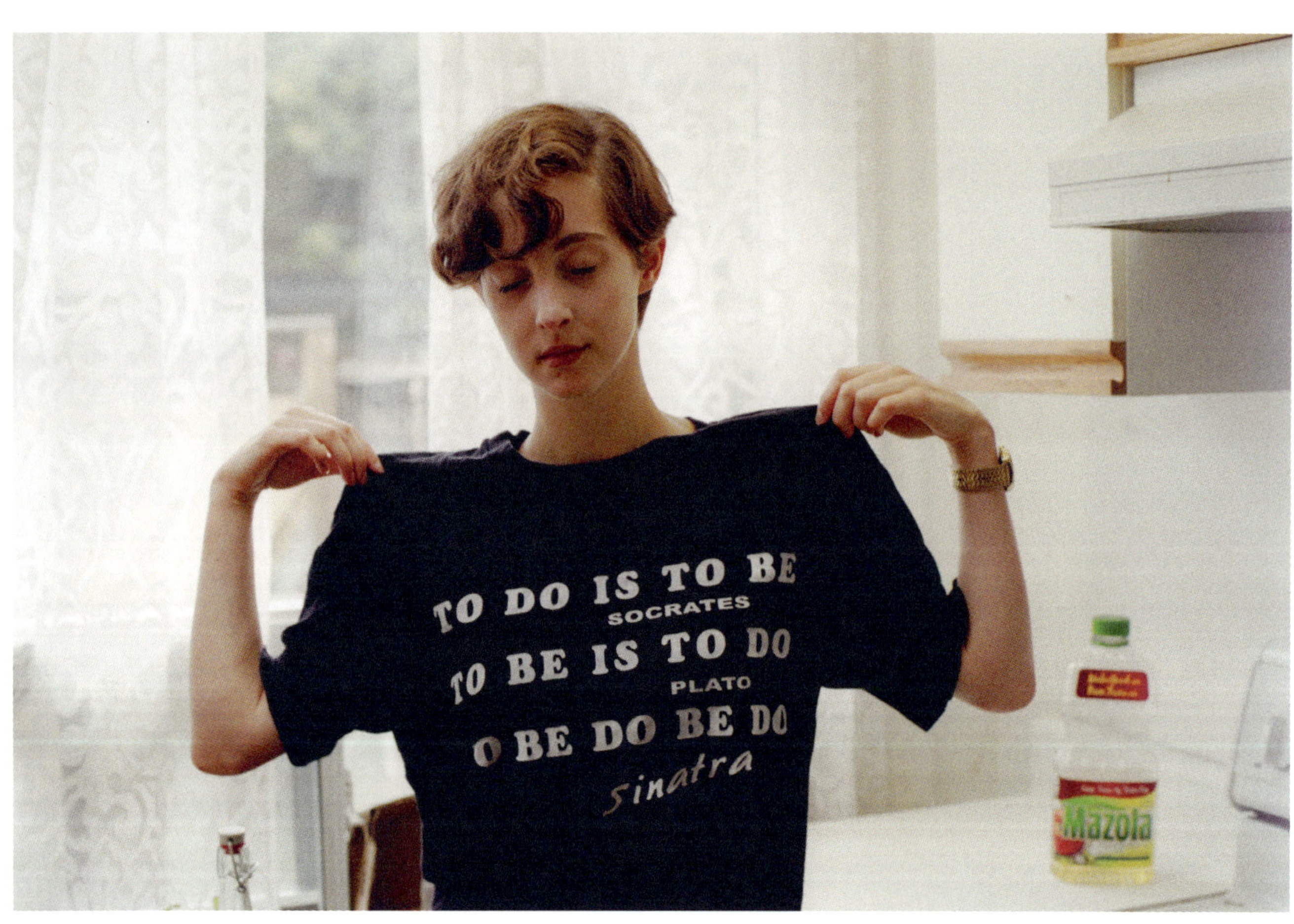
TO DO IS TO BE
SOCRATES
TO BE IS TO DO
PLATO
O BE DO BE DO
sinatra
Mazola

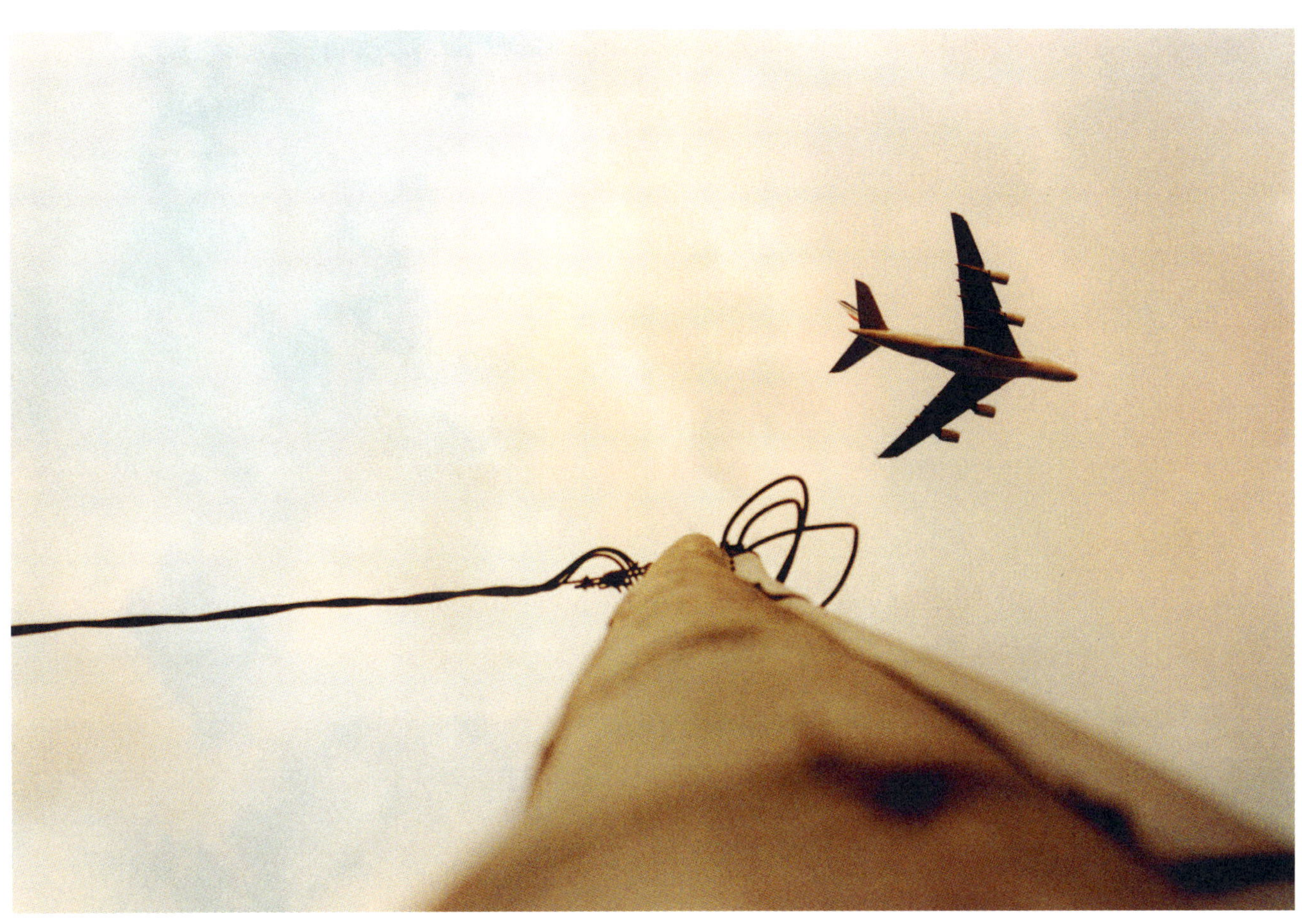

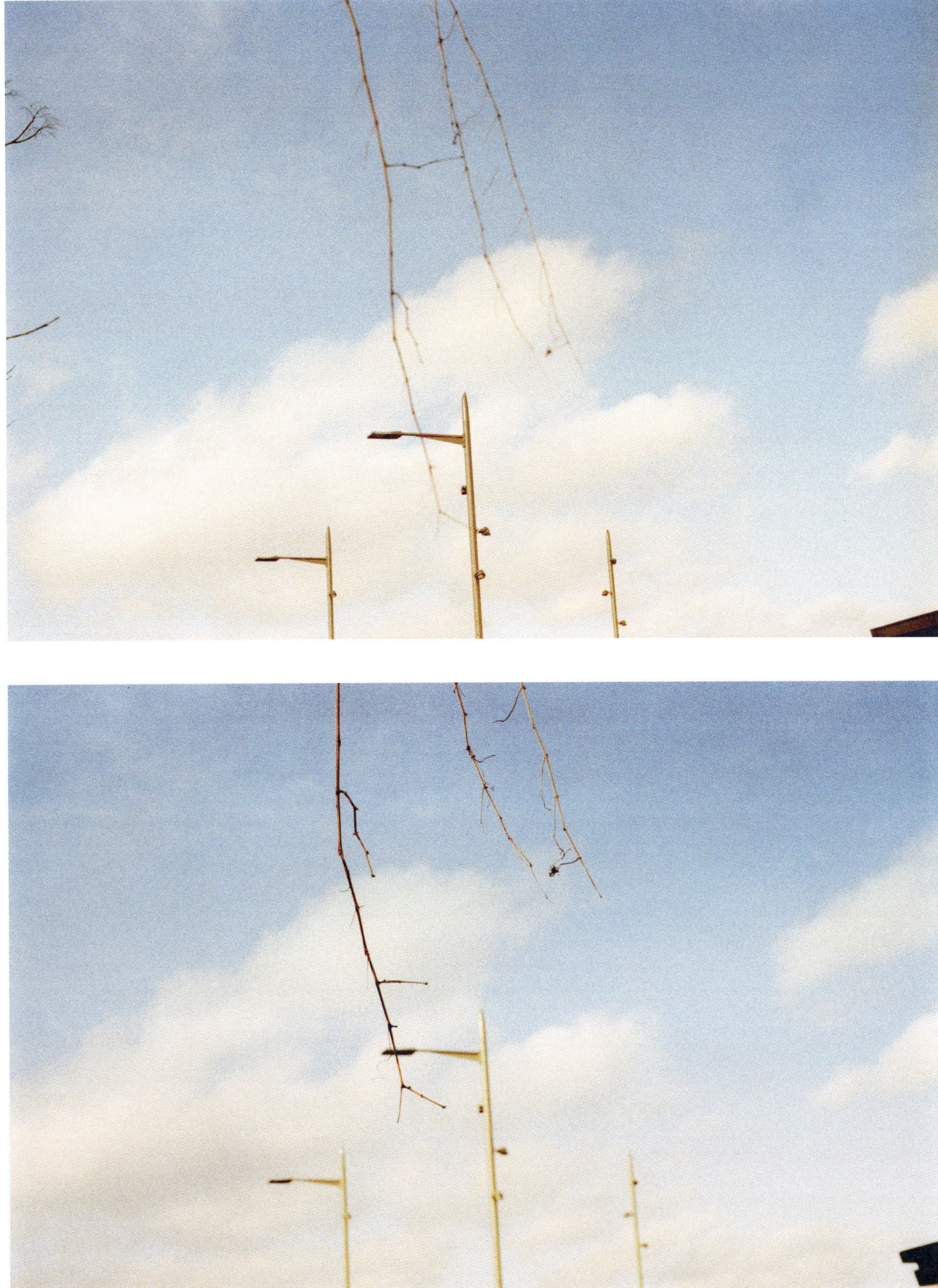

INDEX of Images

In order from cover image.
Pages with multiple images are listed as top image first.

Special thanks to:

Jenni Crain

Alis Atwell, Siobhan Bohnacker, Jenna Bouma, Alison Boyd, Cole Boyd, Steven Brahms, Kelsey Burns, Asger Carlsen, Don Gatanis, Peter Funch, John Kremer, Ryan Lowry, Heather McKenna, Hans Munk, Andrew Musson, Boru O'Brien O'Connell, Charlotte O'Donnell, Justine O'Malley-Jones, Julien Raffinot, Alexa Volkov, Clasien Zodenkamp, V1 Gallery

Adam Kremer
Gates To The Garden

First Edition, 2017
© Adam Kremer
© At Last Books

Introduction by Jenni Crain.
Additional texts by Adam Kremer.
Art Direction & Design by Hans Munk.
Printed by Kopa.

Published by **At Last Books**
www.atlastbooks.com

ISBN: 978-87-999667-2-1

At
Last
Books